Praise for *Appointment in Jerusalem*

It was my great privilege to know Derek and Lydia Prince for many years. Lydia Prince was a lover of Israel, a compassionate and tender woman who adopted nine daughters and whose demeanor was as bold as a lioness.

On one occasion, when I was visiting Lydia and Derek in Florida, Lydia asked me if I would like some tea. I responded, "Yes, I would love some ice tea."

Lydia, who was Danish, looked straight at me and responded, "In my home we do not boil water and then mix it with ice to make it cold; we do not add sugar and then fill it full of lemons. We have hot tea, if you would like some."

I responded, "I would love to have some hot tea." She smiled, left the room, and minutes later produced the hot tea.

When Derek was ministering in my church, Lydia sat on the front row like a five-star general. One woman before service asked Lydia, "How are your children?"

Lydia responded, "Do you really want to know?"

The woman was trapped. "Yes, I would love to hear about your children." Lydia took her by the hand and sat her down on the pew beside her for a forty-five-minute review of how and where her nine daughters were doing. That was Lydia.

She and Derek are in heaven today walking the streets of the New Jerusalem, looking down on ancient Jerusalem in Israel, knowing that soon we shall all be there together.

—John Hagee
Senior Pastor
Cornerstone Church
San Antonio, Texas

I was overwhelmed by the dramatic power of *Appointment in Jerusalem*. Lydia struck me as one of the truly authentic modern heroines. Few women have ever demonstrated such courage, compassion, and commitment. This combination of wartime struggle, family separation, and love between a mature woman, Lydia, and the younger man, Derek Prince, gives *Appointment in Jerusalem* a broad international appeal. The story made me smile, cry, and applaud.

—*Al Kasha*
Two-time Academy-Award-winning Composer,
Author, and Minister

Derek and Lydia Prince mentored many young believers who came to faith during the Jesus Movement, including my wife Susan and me. The special way this book captures and presents Lydia Christensen Prince's heroic and pioneering faith had a galvanizing and lasting influence in our lives. We pray that this anniversary edition impacts thousands of young believers in a similar way today.

—*Gary P. Bergel*
President, Intercessors for America

There are two books which have profoundly affected my spiritual walk. The first was *The Hiding Place*, the second *Appointment in Jerusalem*. Lydia's intimate relationship with Jesus, the way she was led by the Holy Spirit, her devotion to prayer, her sacrifices, and her walk by faith were awe-inspiring. It is a life-changing book.

—*Ann Perdue*
Film Producer, The Brightlight Foundation

This true, heartwarming story of a valiant single woman, who gave up everything to be obedient to the call of God on her life, will inspire and challenge anyone who reads it. Lydia Prince was my mentor and my friend. I can recommend this book to young and old without any reservations.

—*Mrs. Alice Basham*
Wife of the late Don Basham,
Pastor, Author, and International Speaker

Derek & Lydia Prince

APPOINTMENT
In
JERUSALEM

A True Story of Faith, Love, and the Miraculous Power of Prayer

WHITAKER
HOUSE

APPOINTMENT IN JERUSALEM:
A True Story of Faith, Love, and the Miraculous Power of Prayer
Revised and Updated Edition

Derek Prince Ministries
P.O. Box 19501
Charlotte, North Carolina 28219-9501
www.derekprince.org

ISBN: 978-1-60374-574-1
eBook ISBN: 978-1-60374-672-4
Printed in the United States of America
© 1975, 2005 Derek Prince Ministries, International

1030 Hunt Valley Circle
New Kensington, PA 15068
www.whitakerhouse.com

Library of Congress Cataloging-in-Publication Data for Hardcover Edition
Prince, Lydia (Lydia Christensen), 1890–1975.
Appointment in Jerusalem : a true story of faith, love, and the miraculous power of prayer / by Derek and Lydia Prince.— Rev. and updated ed.
p.   cm.
Summary: "The true story of Lydia Christensen Prince's journey from affluent Danish schoolteacher to 'mother' of abandoned Jewish and Arab orphans in Jerusalem"—Provided by publisher.
ISBN-13: 978-0-88368-794-9 (trade hardcover : alk. paper)
ISBN-10: 0-88368-794-1 (trade hardcover : alk. paper) 1. Prince, Lydia (Lydia Christensen), 1890-1975. 2. Pentecostals—Denmark—Biography. 3. Jerusalem—Description and travel. I. Prince, Derek. II. Title.
BX8762.Z8P75 2005
275.694'420824092—dc22   2005024620

7 8 9 10 11 12 13 14 15 **Ⱳ** 30 29 28 27 26 25 24 23

CONTENTS

FOREWORD

by Elizabeth Sherrill

One of the most unforgettable experiences of my life was to spend time in Derek and Lydia's home during the writing of *Appointment in Jerusalem*. "Home" is indeed the word for that sunlit house in Ft. Lauderdale. It was the residence of a *family*, founded and nourished by two people who had no biological children of their own, but were mother and father in the truest and most enduring sense of those words. Daughters, sons-in-law, and grandchildren living nearby were in and out of the house; the phone rang with keeping-in-touch calls from farther away; letters came from children in far-flung countries overseas. The closeness and mutual caring of this collection of very diverse individuals was palpable in the very air of the house.

My working relationship with this couple was unique to the Princes, too. On the one hand was Derek, preacher, biblical scholar, analytical thinker, and author of widely read teaching books, confronting an entirely different discipline. For his first (and alas only!) narrative book, he had to lay aside the overview, objectivity, and logical structure that were his strengths, and follow from the viewpoint of a single individual a stumbling, step-by-step human drama, letting the teaching emerge from the events, rather than using events to illustrate a teaching. The excitement Derek felt at entering this new world and the speed with which he grasped and mastered new techniques made each day with him an adventure and a source of wonder.

As for Lydia, there were three challenges. The first was to get her to think back over the past. For Lydia, in her 80s, the only important time was the future, where God's wondrous workings continually unfolded. And having wrenched her attention to bygone days, the next effort was to get her to recall what she called "the small stuff"—the tiny, inconsequential physical details quite unimportant to these divine workings, but essential in bringing the past to life for others.

Hardest of all was for this lady, born in a "proper" upper-class nineteenth century European home, to endure the kind of personal questions we had to ask. I remember her indignation when, to get the historical setting right, I insisted on knowing her age. And I remember the grace with which she finally acceded, for the sake of the book she hoped would "reach people," to all these assaults on her natural inclinations. In letting Derek and me share the years of testing that shaped her ministry, she let us meet the remarkable woman that not even her children knew at so intimate a level.

Lydia's sensitivity about her age stemmed, I believe, from her consciousness that she was twenty-five years older than her husband. It was not a fact that I think ever entered Derek's mind. For that was the other great delight of being in that home. Derek and Lydia were a team, certainly, partners in ministry, "yoked together" as he writes, "for service." But more than that, those of us who knew them were quickly aware, they were lovers. This was a love-match, a romance that over thirty years only grew sweeter and deeper, a union of two people who became one in a way few husbands and wives ever have.

—*Elizabeth Sherrill*
Author, *All the Way to Heaven*

AUTHOR'S NOTE

In the course of Lydia's story, reference is made to various currencies—Danish kroner, British pounds, Palestinian pounds, U.S. dollars. In most places, for the reader's convenience, amounts in other currencies have been expressed in their approximate equivalent in U.S. dollars at that time.

All biblical quotations in this story are taken from the King James Version. However, in "A Drama in Three Acts" some quotations are taken from the *New American Standard Bible*.

To avoid possible offense or embarrassment, the names of some of the persons in the story have been changed.

PREFACE TO
ORIGINAL EDITION

This is the story of three years in the life of a most remarkable woman, who also happens to be my wife. They are the years that took her from a life of physical comfort and professional fulfillment to one of danger, poverty, and estrangement from everything and everyone she held dear. A schoolteacher at the top of her profession, she left her native Denmark—that clean and lawful land—to travel alone and penniless to a primitive and violent place. The place was Jerusalem; the time, the opening battle of the long war between Jew and Arab that is still going on.

There Lydia endured the rigors of hunger and thirst, the dangers of street fighting and siege. And there she discovered what all of us seek and so few find: joy, peace, perfect security—no matter what the external condition of our lives.

Moving out into the realm of spiritual exploration a generation ahead of her time, Lydia became a pioneer of the charismatic movement, which has since been recognized by many as the most positive and hopeful factor in today's world. In the face of the mounting pressures and tensions that now confront us all, her story points the way to answers that will stand the test of the twentieth century.

I know this has been so for me. Lydia and I met and married in Jerusalem toward the end of World War II. Having graduated in Britain from Eton College and Cambridge University, I had at that time held a fellowship at King's College, Cambridge, for six years. But a completely new phase of my education began the day I climbed the outside stairs of a gray stone house and met the blue-eyed Danish woman whom a houseful of Jewish and Arab children called *Mama*.

In that house I met the Holy Spirit, not as one Person of a theological doctrine called the Trinity, but as a present, potent, daily reality. I watched Lydia set out plates on the table when there was no food to put on those plates, knowing that by the time we sat down to eat, God would have provided the meal. I watched her rebuke fever and sickness in the children and saw the sickness depart.

Above all I watched the Spirit nourish her, lead her, and support her all day, every day, through the pages of the Bible. I had studied the Scriptures in their original languages, analyzed their historic components, pondered their exegesis. Lydia let them speak to her heart. "I read the gospel of John," she once said, "like a love letter."

In thirty years of marriage I have learned from Lydia that prayer that springs from this kind of intimacy with the Bible is not a subjective thing but a force in the world—the most powerful there is. A while ago our daughter Johanne remarked to her son Jonathan that Lydia was praying about something. "Well, if Granny's praying about it," Jonathan commented, "I suppose that settles it."

To me the fascinating thing in all this is that for the first thirty-five years of her life, Lydia, in her own opinion and everybody else's, was the last person on earth to whom this sort of thing could happen. An intellectual, a bit of a snob, a well-to-do young woman who delighted in new clothes and dancing and all the pleasures of the cultured world into which she was born, she had read the Bible only when it was required reading for a course in teachers college.

The route by which this twentieth-century agnostic discovered the reality of God is so full of guidelines for us all, so full of practical help for every person embarked on this quest today, that from the start I urged Lydia to get her experiences on paper.

But Lydia has always been too busy living life to write about it. Gradually I realized that if the story were to be told, I must be the one to tell it. By now I was intimately acquainted with all the places, and almost all the persons, who figured in these events; thus I could reconstruct both scenes and personalities from firsthand knowledge.

This is Lydia's story. I have tried, insofar as a man may do this, to enter into her mind and emotions, to portray events in her own words as she experienced them at the time—not seeking to gloss over struggles and weaknesses, but letting the real woman speak for herself.

However, there is another character in this book—in a sense the true heroine—the city of Jerusalem. In these chapters Lydia paints Jerusalem as she first knew it in the decade that followed four hundred years of Turkish domination, a very different place from the city now familiar to tourists. Then, in the Epilogue[1] at the end of the book, I become the speaker, attempting to lift the veil of the future and sketch a picture of what lies ahead for Jerusalem—and for us all. For the key to the world's history lies in this single city.

The things I write about may happen in the 1970s, the '80s, the '90s, and beyond. Scripture does not say when; it only assures us that all will take place exactly as foreshown in prophecy. It is our prayer that through this book Lydia and I will be able to share with you the urgency we feel about the coming days in this city, and the love she inspires in everyone who takes seriously the bidding of God to "pray for the peace of Jerusalem."

—Derek Prince

---

1. Editor's note: This is now the Appendix.

1

TIKVA

The last glow of the setting sun had faded from the sky behind me, leaving the streets of Jerusalem dark and empty. The silence was broken only by the scuff of my shoes against the stones. The damp, wintry air felt raw against my cheek. Instinctively, I clutched closer to me the bundle that I carried.

At length, with a sigh of relief, I turned down a stone staircase that led to a basement door. Cradling the bundle with my left arm, I reached my right hand into my coat pocket and pulled out a heavy iron key. The key turned in the lock with a rasping sound that echoed across the empty courtyard. Stepping hastily inside, I inserted the key again from the other side, and the same rasping sound told me that the door was safely locked once more.

I groped my way across the room to the bed against the opposite wall and set my burden down upon it. Beside the bed there was a wooden dresser. Feeling across its top with my hand, I picked up a box of matches and struck one. Its small flame revealed a kerosene lamp that stood on the dresser. I struck a second match and lit the lamp.

It illuminated an austere room, paved with bare flagstones. The walls, too, were of stone and—except for a picture calendar hanging above the bed—they were equally bare. Apart from the bed and dresser, there were only three other pieces of furniture—a table and chair against one wall, and a wicker trunk under the window. The window was fitted with heavy iron bars—mute testimony to the fear that drove each citizen to make a fortress of his home.

I turned again to the bundle on the bed. Inside the coarse black shawl lay a baby girl, her tiny body partly covered by a stained cotton undershirt. The skin of her face, like delicate yellow parchment, was stretched tight across the cheekbones and burned like fire to my touch. The black hair, moist with perspiration, was pressed against the temples. Out of deep sockets, two black eyes gazed momentarily up at me—and then closed.

I turned back another fold of the shawl and drew out a baby's bottle containing a few ounces of tepid milk. As I did so, a crumpled scrap of paper fell out and fluttered to the floor. Gently I inserted the bottle into the baby's mouth and waited for a response. At first the physical effort of drinking seemed to be too great for her, but after a while she began to suck slowly at the nipple.

I picked up the scrap of paper from the floor and smoothed it out. It contained three lines carefully written in capitals:

TIKVA COHEN—BORN IN JERUSALEM—
4TH DECEMBER 1927

Automatically I glanced at the calendar above the bed. It was Friday, December 28, 1928. I could hardly believe it—the baby was already more than a year old! Had I been left to judge only by her size and weight, I would have said that she was less than half that age.

As the baby continued to suck, I glanced around the room. I needed a place to protect her from the damp air and the chill of the stones. What could I use? My eyes fell on the wicker trunk beneath the window. That would do! But I needed something to line it with. Quickly I opened the drawers of the dresser and pulled out all the pieces of underwear and other soft clothing that I could find. With these I lined the bottom and sides of the trunk, making it as soft and inviting as I could. I left the lid raised and leaning against the bars of the window.

By this time the baby had stopped sucking and seemed to be asleep. I gently eased her out of the cotton vest. Then I took off the blue woolen sweater that I was wearing and wrapped it around her body two or three times. As I laid her in the trunk, she whimpered momentarily but soon fell silent again. Her breath came in quick, shallow gasps, and the fever sent intermittent shudders through her body.

Where could I turn for help? Mentally I pictured the dark, empty streets of Jerusalem, haunted by fear and suspicion. Every door was locked, every window shuttered. There was no telephone to summon an ambulance or a doctor. I was shut up in that bare room with a dying child.

My eye was attracted to the Book lying open beneath the lamp on the dresser. The Bible. Was there a message in it for me at that moment? The passage to which it was opened was in the epistle of James. I began to read down the page and was arrested at two verses underlined in green:

Is any sick among you? let him call for the elders of the church; and let them pray over him, anointing him with oil in the name of the Lord: and the prayer of faith shall save the sick, and the Lord shall raise him up.   (James 5:14–15)

Anointing...with oil... I repeated the words slowly to myself. Oil was one thing that was available. To be sure, I was no "elder." But I was alone, without any other source of help. Surely it was better to do what I could than to do nothing at all!

I opened the closet in the wall where I kept my few items of food. I took out a bottle and held it up against the light. The contents gleamed dully, halfway between green and gold. It was pure olive oil from the Judean hills—the same kind that through bygone centuries had been poured in holy anointing upon the kings and prophets of Israel.

Holding the bottle of oil in my left hand, I knelt on the stone floor in front of the wicker trunk. The baby's breathing was becoming more and more labored. The air around us had become strangely damp. A cold shiver went through me. I was face-to-face with an invisible presence—the presence of Death.

In an effort to strengthen my faith, I repeated aloud the words that I had just read from the Bible, "The prayer of faith shall save the sick,...the Lord shall raise him up"! With a hand that trembled slightly, I tipped a few drops of oil onto the fingers of my right hand and lightly drew them across the baby's forehead.

"In Your name, Lord Jesus!" I whispered. "She's Your little sister—one of Your own people. For Your name's sake, Lord, I ask You to heal her!"

After some minutes I opened my eyes. Was it my imagination, or were the feverish shudders less intense? I placed my hand against the baby's cheek. Burning!

I closed my eyes and began to pray again. "Lord, it was You who brought me here. It was You who told me to leave my country and come to Jerusalem. Lord, let these people know that there is power in Your name and that You do hear and answer prayer."

Time stood still. On my knees in front of the trunk I alternately prayed and watched the baby for any change in her condition. At times her breathing seemed easier, but her skin still burned with the fever. Every now and then I would observe her black eyes, sunken unnaturally deep in their sockets, gazing solemnly up at me.

Eventually my knees became stiff and cold from the pressure of the stone floor. I rose and walked to and fro across the room, still praying. After an hour or two I decided that I would gain nothing by staying on my feet any longer. Even if I could not sleep, it would be wiser to protect myself from the dampness of the room by getting into bed.

Before extinguishing the lamp, I held it over the baby to see if there was any change. For the time, at least, her shuddering had ceased. She seemed to be sleeping. But her skin still burned with the fever. How much longer could that tiny frame hold out against it? Finally I blew out the lamp, climbed into bed, and pulled the covers up around my neck.

As I lay there in the dark, I began to go over in my mind the strange series of events that had brought me to Jerusalem. With the eye of memory I could see the map of Denmark that hung on the classroom wall where, until six months ago, I had been teaching geography. Like a jagged, flint arrow, the promontory of Jutland stabbed into the Skagerrak. In the lee of Jutland, to the east, nestled the two islands of Fyn and Sjælland, separated by the narrow strip of water called Store Bælt.

On the east shore of Store Bælt, and on the southwest corner of Sjælland, stood the town of Korsør. With eager longing, my mind filled in the details. How they contrasted with Jerusalem! The streets were clean and brightly lit. On either side stood rows of trim brick houses with red-tiled roofs and white-painted eaves. Once again I could hear the shrill voices of the children singing the song that all Danish children learn at school.

I Danmark er jeg født,
Der har jeg hjemme....

In Denmark I was born,
And there my home is....

2

SOREN

It was two years earlier—December 1926. The slanting rays of the northern sun were reflected in a deep orange glow from the classroom windows. I said goodnight to the janitor, who stood waiting to close the iron gates of the schoolyard, mounted my bicycle, and set out on the familiar road that wound its way back to the center of Korsør.

Five or six minutes of brisk cycling brought me to the western side of the city, just a few hundred yards from the shore of Store Bælt. I parked my bicycle in the courtyard of a large, red brick building and climbed the stairs to my apartment on the second floor. In the open doorway Valborg, my maid, stood ready to greet me, drying her hands on her red-and-white-checkered apron.

"Welcome home!" she said, reaching up to help me off with my fur-lined coat.

In the dining room my eye lingered with satisfaction on the table set for the evening meal. The crystal chandelier cast its soft gleam over the glistening silverware and the starched damask tablecloth. While I slipped for a moment into the bedroom, Valborg lit the candles and set a bowl of steaming soup at my place.

As I sipped my soup, Valborg lingered beside my chair. After spending most of the day by herself in the apartment, she was ready for conversation.

"That's your last week of school finished for this year," she said, "and tomorrow night is the teachers' dance."

"That reminds me," I replied. "You won't need to prepare a meal for me tomorrow evening. Mr. Wulff is taking me out to dinner before the dance."

Valborg was obviously interested in this arrangement. She liked Soren Wulff—and so did I. But...

"I'll be going home to Brønderslev over Christmas," I said, to change the subject. "You won't need to do anything here in the apartment while I'm away."

At the close of the meal I lit the slim cheroot that Valborg had discreetly placed beside my coffee cup. Then I picked up the cup and carried it into the living room. Still puffing at my cheroot, I settled back in a deep armchair that stood in one corner and allowed my gaze to travel slowly around the room. Against the opposite wall the well-polished walnut case of the piano faintly reflected the yellow and bronze shades of the Wilton carpet. The wall behind it was covered with a paper in shades of olive green that gave the impression of tapestry and blended well with the gold brocade curtains. The wall at my left hand was covered from floor to ceiling by a bookcase, on whose shelves rows of books alternated with Dresden china figures and vases and bowls of German crystal.

For a minute or two I consciously savored the comfort and elegance of it all. I asked myself, as I had often done before, "Is there anyone in the world more fortunate than I am?" At the age of thirty-six I had already attained the goal that I had set for myself as a teacher. In addition to my certificates in standard subjects such as history, geography, Danish, and English, I had been one of the first teachers in the nation to complete a special postgraduate course in domestic science, with emphasis on recent discoveries in the field of nutrition. As a result, I had been appointed director of domestic science in one of Denmark's newest and best-equipped schools. My department was now being used by the educational authorities as a pattern for the establishment of similar departments in other schools throughout the nation.

Over the past ten years I had taught in various towns of Denmark, but none suited me so well as Korsør, with its beautiful situation on Store Bælt and yet within easy reach of Copenhagen. My salary was a good one, and in addition I had received a generous legacy after my father's death two years before.

Over and above all this there was Soren Wulff—the teacher who was taking me out the next evening. Soren and I had been close friends in teachers college, having many loves in common—dancing, skating, Mozart, Kierkegaard. After graduating we had taught in separate schools for nearly ten years. Now—as fate would have it—we were together again in Korsør. During the past term I had gradually become aware of a new seriousness in Soren's attitude toward me. I was almost sure that tomorrow night he was going to ask me to marry him. Why was I afraid to be faced with that question?

By nature, by training, by profession, Soren was one thing first and fore-most: a teacher. His whole life centered around his work. Marriage to him would be marriage to his profession. Since I was also a teacher, it was seem-ingly an ideal combination. Certainly, if I wished to marry and have children, I could not afford to wait much longer!

And yet...there was a finality about it that frightened me. Why should I have to fight that inner reservation? Was there still something that was needed to make our lives complete? During the past year I had turned this question over in my mind a hundred times, but I had never been able to find an answer. Indeed, I had no idea where to look for one.

At six o'clock the next evening I put the finishing touches to my coiffure and lingered for a moment in front of my mirror. My long, blond hair was caught up in four braids and interlaced over my head, the way Soren liked it. The blue silk dress that Valborg had ironed for me added an extra shade of blue to my eyes. Blue was Soren's favorite color, and mine, too. We had so much in common...

My reverie was interrupted by a loud knock. Quickly pulling on my white fur cape, I opened the door. Soren's athletic figure was set off by a beautifully fitting suit of tails, his scrupulously groomed brown hair smelling faintly of bay rum.

"I have a taxi waiting downstairs," he said as he caught my outstretched hand in both of his.

At the restaurant Soren led the way to a table for two in the far corner. "I've been looking forward to this evening for two weeks," he said. "Do you realize that it's twelve years almost to the day since we first danced together?"

The waiter came to take our orders, and our conversation turned to the events of the term that had just ended. Soren was lively and entertaining as usual, but I caught a note of tension in his voice. Eventually the waiter cleared the table, leaving only our coffee and brandy in front of us.

Soren took a quick sip from his coffee; then he raised his eyes and looked me full in the face. "Lydia," he said, "I had a special reason for asking you to have dinner with me tonight—and I have an idea that you already know what that reason is." He paused while his green eyes searched mine. "Lydia, will you marry me?"

I felt the color mounting to my cheeks and my heart pounding so loud that I was sure everyone in the room could hear it. This was the moment that I had been expecting, and yet I had no answer ready. I opened my mouth to answer him, wondering what I was going to say.

"Thank you, Soren," I heard myself say. "That's the nicest compliment that anyone has ever paid me. But..."

"But what?"

"Soren, I'm not free to commit myself just now."

"Is there someone else?"

"No, that's not it. I don't know anyone that I like or respect more than you." I struggled to explain myself, but no words came.

Leaning forward across the table, Soren began to speak again. His words tumbled over one another. He painted a picture of what the future held for us together, the interests and activities that we could share, the way that our careers would blend and complement each other. Finally he paused, waiting for my response.

"I know how much your career as a teacher means to you, Soren," I began, "and for that reason I'm all the more flattered that you're willing to share your future with me. But I'm afraid that things might not work out the way you describe."

"Why not, Lydia?"

"You see, I'm not as settled about my future as you are, Soren. Before I can commit myself in the way you ask, there's something I have to settle first."

"What's that?"

"I know this must sound foolish..." I was still groping for words. "But I keep asking myself, Is there something more to life than just a career and an apartment—and nice furniture—and a pension at the end of it all? I don't know. But when my father died two years ago, I couldn't help wondering, Is that really the end—or is there something more?"

"Do you mean something to do with religion?"

"Perhaps that may be it—though I don't like that word *religion*."

Poor Soren! I could see that he was as bewildered as I was. He took several quick sips of his coffee.

"Forgive me for giving you such a foolish answer," I replied. "I'm like a person trying to decide the best way to a place when I've never been there myself."

We both sat silent for a few moments while I searched for a way to relieve the tension. Finally I reached my hand across the table and took his. "Would you mind if we went on to the dance now, and I'll try to do a better job of explaining myself later on?"

When the dance ended, Soren escorted me back to my apartment, and I invited him up for a final cup of coffee. He was the first to return to the theme of our conversation in the restaurant.

"Lydia, if you want me to go with you to church," he said, "I'm willing to do that."

"No, Soren," I replied, "I wouldn't ask that of you. I've been a good Lutheran all my life, but that hasn't answered my questions. My first year here in Korsør I went to church every Sunday, but I used to come out each time feeling more confused and frustrated than when I went in, so in the end I gave up."

"Well, then," Soren said, "why don't you try going to the Evangelical Mission down by the harbor? I'm sure our dear librarian, Miss Sonderby, would be happy to take you there with her."

Momentarily I pictured Kristine Sonderby as I often saw her on her way to the Mission. A shapeless, black felt hat overshadowed a fringe of gray hair and a pair of thick, black-rimmed spectacles. From the side pocket of her bulky, black leather purse protruded a Bible and a hymnbook—both bound in black. From her hat to her high-button boots, the recurrent motif was black. "Salvation," as Kristine Sonderby represented it, was certainly a melancholy affair—its benefits, whatever they might be, all reserved for some future life. No, that was not what I was looking for!

A few minutes later Soren took his leave. In the doorway he held me for a moment in his arms—then turned and descended the stairs without another word.

After he had gone, I tried not to think anymore about what had passed between us, but the faint fragrance of his pomade lingered in the apartment as a reminder. How real and warm he had felt as he held me in his arms!

By comparison, my quest for the unknown "something" that would make life complete seemed vague and shadowy.

———————

By ten o'clock the next morning I was seated in a first-class compartment on a train headed northward to the town of Brønderslev, where I had been born and where my mother still lived. I had not slept well the previous night, and my head was throbbing. The journey took six hours, which gave me plenty of time to think—more than I really wanted. My mind kept returning to my conversation with Soren the night before. I still did not understand my own behavior.

A voice inside reproached me: "You've thrown away your chance of happiness! You could have had marriage and a home and security. Now you've lost all that!"

I turned my gaze to the window, trying to fix my mind on the scenes that passed outside, but the voice continued: "And what have you got to put in place of marriage? Nothing! You'll end up just a typical old-maid teacher, like Miss Sonderby!"

Again and again I went over my conversation with Soren. As I remembered each thing I had said to him, the reproachful voice within me asked, "Why did you say that? You didn't really mean it. You didn't even know what you were saying."

After a while the rhythmic clatter of the train wheels took up the question like a refrain: *Why did you say that? Why did you say that? Why did you say that?*

I lit a cheroot and took quick puffs at it, but it did not provide the relief I needed. I got up and began to walk up and down in the corridor of the train. But still the wheels pursued me relentlessly: *Why did you say that?*

Only with great effort was I able to turn my mind away from Soren to the family reunion that awaited me in Brønderslev. My father had been a successful builder and had played an important role in developing the town. After his death two years earlier, Mother had moved into a large building known as "the castle" that had been constructed by Father in the town center, only a few hundred yards from the railway station. Here Mother occupied a four-bedroom apartment on the second floor.

It was a family tradition that we should all gather at home for Christmas. My eldest sister, Kezia, would be coming from the island of Fyn with her husband, Knud, and four children. My second sister, Ingrid, was married to an officer in the Danish Army with a large estate about fifty miles from Brønderslev. They had no children. I was the "baby" of the family and the only one still unmarried.

On arrival at Brønderslev I quickly picked out a tall, slim figure with a starched white cap awaiting me on the platform—Mother's maid, Anna. "Welcome home, Miss Lydia!" she said, relieving me of my suitcase. "Your mother's been counting the hours until you came." With her long strides Anna led the way across the main square to "the castle."

Mother was waiting to meet me in the hallway. "Welcome home, my little girl!" she said, taking me in her arms. For her I was always a little girl—though now in my mid-thirties.

Since Father's death Mother had retained the traditional black of a widow, but her long silk dress, relieved by white lace collar and cuffs, was not without elegance. Her blond hair had taken on an ashen tinge that gave her added dignity.

Mother and I had supper alone together. She was always eager to hear about my work at the school and proud of each promotion that I achieved. Soon my sisters arrived with their families. As usual their first question was, "Has anyone proposed to you yet?" But for some reason I said nothing about Soren.

The following day was Christmas Eve, in Denmark the time of the chief celebrations. In the afternoon there was a brief church service. Mother was a "good Lutheran" and there were two occasions each year when she attended church—Christmas Eve and Easter.

On our way to the church Mother began to tell me about their new pastor. "He's such a nice man," she said. "Everyone likes him!"

"By that you mean, Mother, that he preaches nice short sermons!"

"Well, yes, that's true. I never did like long sermons. Besides, he plays whist. He comes to see me every Tuesday, and we have a game of cards together."

That afternoon the pastor lived up to his reputation. The service commenced at 3:00 PM, and by 3:45 we were out in the street again. With a sense of duty well done, we made our way back home. There the really serious part of the Christmas celebrations awaited us—the tree, the gifts, the abundance of everything delicious to eat and drink.

At six o'clock we all took our places at the long dining room table. My earliest childhood memories were interwoven with these Christmas traditions. For a moment, in my mind's eye, I saw Father once again, seated at the head of the table, the heavy gold watch chain across his vest reflecting the gleam of the Christmas lights. The older son-in-law, Knud, now took his place.

There was a well-established protocol that governed each phase of our festivities. When everyone was seated, Anna—in the blue uniform she saved for special occasions—opened the double doors that led into the living room. There in the center of the floor stood the Christmas tree. Lighted candles on each branch revealed a heap of gorgeously wrapped gifts piled at the tree's foot. Below the branches were suspended little paper baskets containing candies, chocolates, and marzipan. The children uttered little gasps of wonder as their eyes took in each detail of the scene.

Next Anna lit the long, red candles in the center of the table. Then she withdrew to the kitchen, switching off the electric light as she went. While we waited for Anna to return, my eye moved up and down the table. Apart from a vacant space in front of Knud, every inch was covered with a dish of some kind. In addition to ordinary boiled potatoes there were two dishes of special "caramel" potatoes, three gravy boats, two bowls of red currant jelly, two dishes of red cabbage, a little row of marzipan pigs, and many kinds of pickles. In the center there was a silver dish heaped with apples, oranges, nuts, and green and black grapes.

A few minutes later Anna returned, bearing a large oval platter of the famous Royal Porcelain, which she set down in front of Knud. On it was an immense roast goose, its legs adorned with paper frills, its breast with three little red and white Danish flags. While Knud began to carve the goose, Ingrid's husband opened a bottle of Burgundy.

The dessert consisted of the traditional rice porridge. Buried somewhere in it was a single almond. The person whose helping contained the almond would receive an extra gift, arranged conspicuously on the top of the pile. Everyone searched diligently through his helping, and eventually Ingrid held up the almond, amid sighs of disappointment from the children.

When the huge meal eventually ended, we all moved into the living room. Ingrid's husband took his place at the piano, and the rest of us joined hands in a wide circle around the tree. Then we began to sing the traditional Danish Christmas songs, circling the tree with a sideways dancing step and bowing in unison to the tree as each verse ended.

Of all the familiar songs there was one that always stirred a deeper chord in me than the rest:

My Saviour and my Substitute, all hail!
A crown of thorns the world to Thee assigned;
But, Lord, Thou seest that I have in mind
A crown of roses round Thy cross to bind—
Let me the needed grace and courage find!

As we began to sing these words, I suddenly felt my eyes filling with tears. I quickly bent my head to hide them. What was the matter with me? Momentarily I saw myself back in the restaurant, sitting opposite Soren and struggling to explain my quest for the unknown "something" that was needed to complete our lives. When I raised my eyes again, the people in the living room seemed strangely remote. They were my nearest and dearest, yet somehow I had become a detached spectator, watching events in which I no longer saw any real meaning.

As soon as the singing was over, all the adults started to smoke. The men lit full-size cigars while Mother, my sisters, and I each took a slim cheroot. A lady was not supposed to smoke anything so unrefined as a mere cigarette!

The evening came to its climax with the opening of the gifts. Kezia's eldest boy was given the task of taking gifts from under the tree, reading out the names on them as he did so. Each gift had to be opened and passed around for inspection before the next name was called out. Since there were fifty or sixty gifts, it was nearly midnight before the last gift was opened, and the two youngest children were fast asleep on the floor.

The next afternoon I found myself alone in the living room with Mother. She was sitting in her favorite chair—a rocker—knitting a sweater for one of Kezia's children.

"Tell me, Lydia," she said, "when are you going to get married and settle down?" The rocker kept time with the rhythmic click of the needles in her hands. "You know I'm not getting any younger, and I would love to see you settle down with a husband and a home of your own."

"I do have a home of my own, Mother—a beautiful one. As for marriage, there's something else I need to find out first."

"What's that?" she asked, just as Soren had.

"I'm not sure. But it's something to do with—well, with God." Strange how hard it was to say that word! "I want to find out for myself if God is real— if there is some purpose in life more than just a career and a salary."

"Why, that's exactly how your father began to talk the last year or two!" Mother exclaimed. "He even started attending some kind of meetings in a farmer's home outside town."

"A farmer?" It was hard to picture Father, with his frock coat, vest, and pinstripe trousers, sitting in a farmer's living room.

"Yes. Not at all the kind of people he was used to. In the end I sent them some money. I didn't want your father going there and drinking their coffee for nothing!"

"What else did Father say?"

"Well, I remember him saying one day that money couldn't buy peace of mind.... That was a few weeks before he had his heart attack. You know how suddenly he died."

It all came back in a rush—the telegram, the agonizing train journey, and then entering the room where they had laid out Father's body. I remembered the first intense shock of grief and how that had gradually given way to a sense of peace so real that it was almost like the presence of a person there in the room with me. I remembered, too, the expression on Father's face as he lay there—a look of repose such as I had never seen while he was alive. Surely he had found something in those last weeks of his life. But what?

"What more could there be in life than you already have, Lydia?" Mother's voice broke in upon my memories. "You've done so well in your career, and I know everyone at the school thinks so highly of you. I'm sure that the thing you're missing is a home and children of your own."

"Maybe, Mother, but..." How could I describe that inner restlessness that I could not deny and yet could not explain?

Finally I blurted out, "If there was something special in life that another woman wouldn't do—even if it was difficult or dangerous—that's what I'd like to do!"

I could see the same baffled expression on Mother's face that I had seen a few days before on Soren's. I seemed to express myself worst to those whom I loved most. Was I foolish to go on seeking for something that I could not express in words—even to myself?

3

THE ENCOUNTER

I arrived back in Korsør on Monday, January 3, 1927. School would not reopen for another week. I told Valborg that she need not come back to work before Saturday. I wanted to spend the next few days entirely by myself.

The next morning I went for a long walk by the shore of Store Bælt. A cold, blustery wind whipped the spray up into my face, but I wrapped my scarf more tightly around my throat, bent my head forward, and pressed my body against the wind. Walking thus against the pressure of the elements helped to build in me a sense of determination. No matter what I might have to face, I would not turn back now until I had found the answer to my quest.

Returning to my apartment at lunchtime, I felt no desire to eat. I brewed a strong cup of coffee and lit a cheroot. Then I walked into the living room and scanned the rows of books on the wall opposite me. I read off the names of the authors: Kierkegaard, Oenslaeger, Ibsen, Shakespeare, Dickens, Tolstoy, Plato. I had read them, quoted them, lectured about them—but they offered me no answer now. At the extreme right of the top row my eye rested on a plain volume bound in black.

In teachers college the Bible had been part of a compulsory course on religion and church history. I had read enough of it to pass my examinations, but I had never carried my study further than that. Could there be something in the Bible that I had not found in the other books that I had studied so eagerly? For a moment I hesitated, then I reached up and pulled it down.

Seated in my favorite armchair, I held the Bible unopened for a few moments, wondering where to begin. It seemed reasonable to start with the New Testament. I found the first chapter of Matthew, skimmed quickly through the genealogy of Christ, and read the account of His birth and childhood. The simplicity of Matthew's narrative contrasted forcefully with the elaborate Christmas celebrations in which I had just been taking part.

I read on through the account of Christ's baptism and temptation and the first incidents of His public ministry. Certainly there was a moral beauty that was unmatched by any other book I had read, but I could not see how it related to my present situation. When I reached the Sermon on the Mount, with its opening Beatitudes, I began to read more slowly, pausing at each beatitude to ask myself if it could in any way apply to me.

At the fourth beatitude I suddenly caught my breath: "Blessed are they which do hunger and thirst after righteousness: for they shall be filled" (Matthew 5:6). *Hunger and thirst...* Could this be the very longing that I felt for something I could not express in words? Did I dare to apply these words to myself?

At verse 10 I paused again: "Blessed are they which are persecuted for righteousness' sake." That made no sense. Why should a person be persecuted for seeking after righteousness?

As I continued reading slowly through chapters 5 and 6, I was like a person struggling to find his way through a forest. Overshadowed by interlacing branches, the path was hard to see, but here and there a shaft of sunlight breaking through gave me momentary encouragement. Then, as I reached chapter 7, it was as though I came to a clearing, where the full, uninterrupted rays of the sun came streaming down upon me:

> Ask, and it shall be given you; seek, and ye shall find; knock, and it shall be opened unto you: for every one that asketh receiveth.
>
> (Matthew 7:7–8)

Ask...seek...knock.... Surely I could do that.

I read on, and again the light was clear and bright:

> Enter ye in at the strait gate:...because strait is the gate, and narrow is the way, which leadeth unto life, and few there be that find it.
>
> (Matthew 7:13–14)

Somewhere ahead in the path that I was following, there was a *gate*. Inside, there was a *way* that led to peace and fulfillment. Before I could walk in the *way*, I must first find and enter the *gate*.

I glanced up at the clock on the wall above the piano. It was almost 4:00 PM! More than three hours had passed since I had started reading. Outside, darkness was already coming on. I switched on the light and drew the heavy brocade curtains across the window. I wanted to shut myself in with my own thoughts. I began to walk up and down the room, meditating on the words I had been reading. *Ask...seek...knock....* Certainly I had been *seeking*—for many months. But had I ever *asked?* Whom should I ask? Was Christ speaking of prayer?

In my childhood I had been trained to say the Lord's Prayer each night before I fell asleep. By the age of twelve this had become a monotonous routine. In fact, I recalled that one night I had prayed the Lord's Prayer ten times in succession so as to be free from the burden of praying it for the next nine nights. Apart from this I had joined in the usual congregational prayers and responses in the days when I had attended church. But the thought of praying individually and directly to God—of saying words that were not in the Prayer Book—that was unfamiliar and frightening. Yet I could not get away from Christ's words, "Ask, and it shall be given you." If Christ required me to *ask*, then I could not expect to be *given* anything without asking.

I came to a standstill in front of the armchair in which I had been sitting. Should I kneel? For a moment I was reluctant. Then I bowed my knees to the floor and inclined my body forward over the seat, resting my elbows on the soft velour upholstery. I began mentally, "O God..." But somehow that did not seem right.

Was it necessary to pray *aloud?* The thought of listening to my own voice frightened me. "O God..." I said it aloud. The sound of a voice in the empty room was jarring. I said it again: "O God..." Then a third time: "O God—I do not understand—I do not understand—who is God, who is Jesus, who is the Holy Ghost... But if You will show me Jesus as a living reality, I will follow Him!"

And now in the familiar room, with the sound of the clock ticking in my ears, something took place for which my whole background and education had left me totally unprepared. My mind simply refused to accept what my eyes were seeing. No longer was I looking into the back of the chair. In its place a Person was standing over me. A long white garment covered the Person's feet. Slowly I raised my eyes upward. Above my head I saw two arms outstretched in the attitude of one bestowing a blessing. I raised my eyes further, and then I saw the face of the One who was standing over me. My whole body began to tremble. Involuntarily a word rose to my lips: "Jesus!" But even as I uttered it, He was gone.

Once more I found myself looking down into the chair. In the green velour seat I could see the two hollows left by my elbows. Had there really been a Person standing in front of me just one moment earlier? Or had I been the victim of some brief, incredible hallucination?

I raised my head and looked slowly around the room. Outwardly nothing had changed. Yet there was something in the room that had not been there a minute earlier. I remembered the moment when I entered the room where Father's body lay. The same presence I had felt then was all around me now. The room was actually filled with it. Not only was it round about me, but it was also within me—a deep, untroubled, overflowing peace.

The realization came flooding in upon me—God had actually answered my prayer! He had done exactly what I had asked. He had shown me Jesus. I had seen His garment and His outstretched hands. For one inexpressible moment I had looked into His face. I laid hold upon this one fact: *Christ was alive—eternally, gloriously, radiantly alive!* All the sum of human knowledge paled into insignificance in comparison with this single fact.

Suddenly prayer was no longer an effort. I could not hold back my words of gratitude. "Oh, thank You!" I cried. "Thank You!"

Surging billows of peace flowed over my soul. There seemed to be no way to contain it or to express it. I rose to my feet and began walking to and fro. Every few minutes I was overwhelmed with a fresh realization of what had taken place. "Thank You!" I cried again and again.

I sat down at the piano, searching for some way to give expression to my feelings. I recalled the hymn that had brought tears to my eyes on Christmas Eve. I picked out the tune on the piano. Then I began to sing the words aloud to my own accompaniment:

My Saviour and my Substitute, all hail!
A crown of thorns the world to Thee assigned;
But, Lord, Thou seest that I have in mind
A crown of roses round Thy cross to bind—
Let me the needed grace and courage find!

I sang the words over and over again. Each time my voice became clearer and stronger. There was a river of peace flowing out through my lips in the words that I sang.

I lost track of the time. By turns I knelt at the chair and prayed, then sat at the piano and sang. When I next looked at the clock, it was 10:00 PM. Six hours had passed like so many minutes.

Eventually I undressed and got ready for bed. With the light out I lay in bed, still repeating my words of gratitude, "O God, I thank You! I thank You!" About midnight I slipped gently into dreamless sleep.

Early the next morning I wrapped myself up warmly and went for another long walk by Store Bælt. "How strange!" I said to myself. "Everything looks so fresh and clean... Why didn't I see it yesterday?" Overnight the most familiar objects had gained a new beauty. The white caps of foam, spotlighted here and there by thin shafts of sunlight, the seagulls circling overhead with their harsh calls, the wiry stalks of grass on the sand dunes bending before the blustery wind—all alike bore testimony to the genius of their Creator.

Back in the apartment, I resumed my reading of Matthew's gospel at the point where I had left off the previous evening. The difference was even more dramatic than it had been by Store Bælt. No longer was I struggling to follow an overshadowed path through a forest. I had emerged into full, clear sunlight. I felt myself to be actually present in the scenes that unfolded before me as I read. Through them all there moved the person of Jesus Himself—now not a mere historical figure but a living, present reality.

At noon I prepared myself a hasty snack, then pushed the dishes aside and spread the Bible out on the table before me. Beside it I placed my coffee cup and a freshly lighted cheroot. After a while I became aware of the smoke from the cheroot drifting across the open pages of the Bible. Could it be right, I asked myself, that the smoke should come between me and the Bible? It seemed almost like a veil, obscuring my vision of Christ.

I began to consider the part that smoking played in my life. I had smoked regularly since college. Each morning Valborg awakened me with a cup of coffee and a cheroot. No meal was ever complete unless it was rounded off by the same combination. In moments of pressure or frustration my first reaction was invariably the same—to reach for a cheroot. On the few occasions that Valborg let my supply run out, I would make her stop in the middle of whatever she was doing and run to the store for a packet, scolding her all the while for her lack of foresight.

I glanced down at the cheroot that lay that very moment burning in the ashtray before me. Was it my imagination? Or was there some sinister power in it that held me captive? I felt like a bird fascinated by the eyes of a snake. One thing I knew—by no imaginable exercise of my will could I renounce the attraction that cheroot exercised over me.

Unbidden, a prayer rose to my lips. "God, You know that I can never give that thing up. But if You want to take it from me, I am willing to let it go."

Somewhere below my diaphragm there was a sense of release, as though a knot was being untied. The release found expression in a deep, long sigh that escaped from my lips. For a few minutes I sat limp, my body drained of its strength. Then I picked up the still-burning cheroot and pressed it down into the ashtray, until it broke and crumpled in my hand.

When my legs had regained their strength, I carried the ashtray into the kitchen and emptied it into the garbage. On the kitchen counter I spied an unopened packet of cheroots and cast it also into the garbage. Next I went to the bedroom, pulled another packet out of my purse, and disposed of it in the same manner. Finally I returned to the dining room and resumed my study of the Bible.

Only at the end of the day did I realize that a miracle had taken place. Ten hours had passed without my once reaching for a cheroot! Indeed I had not returned to them even in my mind. For all the interest that I now had in cheroots, they might as well have ceased to exist.

For the next two days a winter storm lashed Korsør. But the raging of the elements outside only heightened by contrast the peace that filled my apartment. I spent most of the time reading on through the Bible. By Friday evening I had reached the gospel of John. The opening verses of the first chapter captivated my attention as no other words had ever done. I read them over and over:

> In the beginning was the Word, and the Word was with God, and the Word was God....In him was life; and the life was the light of men.... And the Word was made flesh, and dwelt among us, (and we beheld his glory, the glory as of the only begotten of the Father).
>
> (John 1:1, 4, 14)

In their combination of grandeur and simplicity, those verses excelled any other piece of literature that I had ever studied.

When I tired of reading, I would take my place at the piano, playing and singing hymns that I had learned in church as a girl. Words and melodies that I had not heard for years returned unbidden to my memory.

From time to time the strangeness of it all would overwhelm me, and I would ask myself, "Am I imagining all this? Or is it really happening to me?" Each time I answered my own questions by two facts so definite that I could not deny them. The first was the abiding peace that filled my inner being and permeated the whole apartment. The second was my miraculous freedom from the cheroots. I knew beyond a shadow of doubt that neither of these results had been achieved by any effort of my will or my imagination.

———————

On Saturday Valborg brought my early-morning cup of coffee to my bedroom.

"Good morning, Miss," she said. "Here's your coffee. I looked everywhere for your cheroots, but I couldn't find them."

"I threw them out," I replied. "I've stopped smoking."

"You've stopped smoking? Whatever for? Have you been sick?"

"I've never felt better in my life! But—well, I don't need my cheroots anymore. You see—something's happened to me..." Hesitantly, groping for the right words, I tried to describe all that had taken place during the past four days.

At the end Valborg stood for some moments without speaking. Then she said, "I never dreamed that things like that could happen to people today. And yet I know it must be real." It was her turn to be embarrassed. "You see...as soon as I opened the door of the apartment this morning, I knew something had changed. There was something here I'd never felt before."

"It's not something, Valborg, it's Someone. It's Jesus! He really is alive—right here and now."

The opening days of the new term passed uneventfully. I saw Soren each day when all the teachers gathered in the common room for the midmorning coffee break, but we did no more than exchange pleasantries. Then, during a free period on Friday afternoon, I was reading a magazine in the teachers' library when I heard Soren's voice behind me. "Am I interrupting the search for truth? Or may I sit down and talk?"

"As a matter of fact," I said, "I've been wanting to share something with you."

"That sounds exciting!" Soren took a seat opposite me.

My heart began to beat faster. I knew it would be harder to explain to Soren than it had been to Valborg. "First of all, Soren, I want to say I'm sorry for giving you such a silly answer the night of the dance. I'm afraid you thought I didn't really appreciate what you said to me."

"You don't have to apologize, Lydia. If this other question is so important to you, you owe it to yourself to seek the answer."

"The thing I wanted to share with you is that—well, I believe I've begun to find the answer."

"You have? In what way?"

I was conscious of Soren's green eyes focused upon me. "For four days last week I was alone in my apartment...reading the Bible and...and praying. And God answered my prayers, Soren! He showed me that Jesus is alive."

"I don't understand."

"Jesus stood right in front of me, Soren. I saw Him with His hands stretched out over me. It only lasted a moment, but it changed everything."

Soren stared at me for a while without speaking. Finally he broke the silence. "Lydia, we're not children, either of us, and we've known each other long enough to be frank. I can see that something has happened to you, but I'm not altogether sure that it has helped you. Don't you think that there's a danger of being too subjective?"

"But, Soren, this wasn't subjective! I didn't just imagine it; I actually saw Jesus in front of me."

"Lydia, I'm not suggesting that you don't feel like that now, but I think you ought to put things in their proper perspective. On your own admission, you were more or less shut away by yourself, and you had been reading the Bible for long periods. I am sure that a psychologist could account in a very reasonable way for everything that happened to you—without introducing such strong emotional overtones."

I was totally unprepared for Soren's answer. His words were like strong gusts of wind threatening to extinguish the little candle of faith that had been kindled within me.

"But, Soren, you don't understand! If only I could explain to you how wonderful it feels to have real peace after all these months of struggling and seeking."

"There you are, Lydia! It's your feelings that you're depending on. But feelings can change. In another month or two you may see things quite differently again."

It was a relief when the class bell rang and we had to separate. As I cycled home from school that evening, my mind was in turmoil. I had looked forward so eagerly to sharing my newfound faith with Soren, but I had failed completely. Instead of believing me, Soren had almost made me doubt my own experience. Obviously I needed some wisdom or power greater than my own if I was to guard my little candle.

As I parked my bicycle in the shed under the stairs, I noticed a piece of printed paper caught in the spokes of the back wheel. I pulled it out, intending to put it into the garbage can in my kitchen, but in the light of my hallway I noticed that the words on it were in English, and this aroused my curiosity.

The paper I held in my hand had originally been a little four-page pamphlet, but the front page, with the opening paragraphs, was missing. The name of the author, given at the end, was Aimee Semple McPherson. I understood that the theme of the pamphlet was the power of prayer. The author related how she had asked God to give her what she called the "spirit of prayer," and described the results that had followed in her life. I was so gripped with the part of the message that was still intact that I read it right through in the hallway, without even taking off my topcoat. Eventually I became aware of Valborg beside me, waiting to help me off with my coat.

When dinner was over and Valborg had bid me good-night, I picked up the pamphlet again. There was a statement in it that I could not dismiss from my thoughts. The author related that at one point she had spent forty hours in continuous prayer. My first inclination was to dismiss this as absurd. And yet if such a thing really were possible, then there must be a dimension in prayer that I had never even dreamed of—much less entered into. What was the "spirit of prayer"?

Eventually I cast myself down in front of the green velour chair that had become my favorite place of prayer. "Lord, I need the same power that woman had," I said. "I ask You to give me the spirit of prayer as You gave it to her." I had half expected some immediate, dramatic response, but none came. "That's what comes," I reproached myself, "of asking for something you don't understand!"

After a few days, however, I realized that the pattern of my life was changing. I began to hunger for prayer, as a person might hunger for food. Excusing myself from the card games and skating parties in which I was usually so active, I arranged each day with one supreme objective in view—to allow the longest possible period of uninterrupted prayer. I told Valborg to prepare only the simplest of meals each evening, and I waited with inward impatience until she had finished her duties and taken her leave.

Once I was left alone, I took my place on my knees in front of the green armchair. Almost invariably, as soon as I tried to start praying, there was something to distract me—a dog barking in the courtyard, a neighbor's child practicing scales on the piano, even the sound of my own clock ticking on the wall. There was also a barrier of self-consciousness inside me. Merely to say words mentally did not seem sufficient. But when I prayed aloud, my own voice sounded strange to me. At times I wondered if my words were reverent enough. At other times they sounded so cold and "churchy."

To break through this double barrier—of distractions from without and self-consciousness within—might take me anything from five minutes to half an hour. But once I had succeeded in pressing through the barrier, it was as though a fountain opened up inside me. Prayer began to flow forth from some source within me, deeper than my conscious mind.

In most cases my prayers on a particular evening seemed to center around some special theme that was not the result of any deliberate choice on my part. This might be my family, or my colleagues, or my pupils. One evening I mentioned by name all the girls in my senior domestic-science class, picturing each girl before me. However, my prayers were not limited to persons whom I actually knew. At times I found myself praying for people in distant lands that were known to me only as areas on a map.

If I could see no way to break through the initial barrier, I would turn to the book of Psalms and read aloud from that. I found special encouragement in the prayers of David. Psalm 42 voiced the thirst of my soul, which I had so long failed to recognize: "As the hart panteth after the water brooks, so panteth my soul after thee, O God" (v. 1). Psalm 51 became my own cry for inward purity: "Purge me with hyssop, and I shall be clean: wash me, and I shall be whiter than snow" (v. 7).

But there was one particular passage to which I returned again and again: "Show me thy ways, O LORD; teach me thy paths. Lead me in thy truth, and teach me: for thou art the God of my salvation; on thee do I wait all the day" (Psalm 25:4–5).

Two weeks earlier I had read about the "strait gate." Then Jesus Himself had opened the gate and led me through it. Inside there was the "narrow way"—a special path in life appointed for me to walk in. Like David, I needed God's help to find this.

During the second half of January I spent almost every evening in prayer like this. Then one Thursday early in February, while I was still struggling through the initial barrier, there was an unexpected knock at my door. Quickly smoothing out the marks of my elbows in the velour seat, I went to the door. My visitor was one of my fellow teachers named Erna Storm. Erna used to ride everywhere on a noisy red motorcycle. For this reason the pupils had nicknamed her "the red storm."

"I came to ask if you would take my duty in the dining hall at lunch-time tomorrow," Erna explained, seating herself in the green velour chair. "I've made an appointment to go with little Elsa Larsen to the doctor. Elsa's eyes are badly crossed, and her parents won't let her be fitted for glasses."

"Whyever not?" I asked.

"Apparently they belong to some religious sect that believes that God heals by prayer, and they're waiting for God to straighten her eyes. In the meanwhile the poor child can't even read what's on the blackboard."

"I never heard of such a thing!" I exclaimed.

"That's not the half of it! They believe in tongues of fire and visions and things like that. 'Pentecostal' they call themselves. Mr. Hansen, the janitor, has a niece who went to one of their meetings, and she said they were rolling on the floor and barking like dogs!"

"Right here in Korsør?"

"Yes, indeed! But that's not the worst! In the summer they take people out into Store Bælt—even good church members—and push them under the water. They call it baptizing them—as if they hadn't been baptized as babies in a proper church service!"

Erna leaned back in her chair and looked around the room. "We don't see much of you these days," she said, "except during school hours. What do you do with yourself in the evenings?"

Erna's question caught me unprepared. "Oh, I'm studying the Bible a lot," I said, "and—praying."

"Studying the Bible and praying?" Erna looked at me in amazement. "Take my advice and don't overdo it! You'll end up like Miss Sonderby—and one person on the staff like her is enough."

After Erna took her leave, I waited until I heard the sound of her motorcycle as she started it up. Then I went back to the living room and knelt down once more. But the barrier seemed harder than ever to break through. Inwardly I kept hearing Erna's words of warning, "Take my advice and don't overdo it!"

4

THE BURIAL

The next evening I was back on my knees again. After struggling in vain to break through the prayer barrier, I turned to the book of Psalms. However, for the first time this, too, proved ineffective. I read two or three psalms aloud, but my voice sounded hollow and lifeless—like echoes reverberating in an empty well.

Eventually I turned to the New Testament and started reading at random, searching for a passage that would give me renewed inspiration. My eye fell on the opening verses of John's first epistle, and I began to read them aloud. I reached the fourth verse: "And these things write we unto you, that your joy may be full."

I read these last words two or three times—*that your joy may be full.* "What is joy?" I asked myself. "Does God really want us to be filled with joy?" As I turned this over in my mind, I became aware of an emotion so intense that its impact was physical. It was actually flowing in warm currents through every part of my body. Unless I could find some way to give expression to it, I would no longer be able to contain myself. I rose to my feet and began walking through the various rooms of the apartment.

In the kitchen my eye fell on a broom standing in one corner. I picked it up and began to waltz around the apartment, holding the broom as if it were my partner at a dance. I tried to tell myself that this was ridiculous and quite out of place in someone who was attempting to pray to God. But still I went on dancing around and around the apartment until I finally collapsed, out of breath, on the sofa.

After about five minutes I had regained my composure sufficiently to continue reading where I had left off. With some difficulty I held my feelings in check until I reached the end of the seventh verse: "...and the blood of Jesus Christ his Son cleanseth us from all sin."

As I came to the last phrase about cleansing from sin, the joy surged up again within me. I was no longer able to pronounce the words that I was reading. I began to stammer, repeating each syllable two or three times. I felt the most intense need to give expression to something within me, and yet I had no words with which to do so, nor did I understand what it was that I needed to express.

I waited a while for the joy to subside, and went back to my reading. I struggled through verse 8 but could scarcely complete verse 9: "If we confess our sins, he is faithful and just to forgive us our sins, and to cleanse us from all unrighteousness." The word *cleanse* brought the joy surging up to the point where again I could not remain seated.

Up to that moment in my life I had never been particularly conscious of any sins that I had committed. In fact, measuring myself by the people round about me, I considered myself to be rather a good person. Yet the words that I had just been reading produced in me a marvelous sense of purity. I could never have believed that a person could feel so clean. My whole inner being seemed to be flooded with the most brilliant light. Looking back over my past, I wondered that I had never realized before how much I needed God's forgiveness. In the light of what I now saw, there were no words adequate to express my thankfulness.

I gave up any further attempts at reading, and retired to bed. As I waited for sleep to come, I knew there were people and situations that I should pray for, but each time I tried to do so, I found myself thanking God instead that I was forgiven and cleansed of all my sins. The more I thanked God for this, the more intense my joy became.

Suddenly I became aware of what seemed to be a voice, inside my chest, speaking words in some foreign language. "Erna was right!" I thought. "You've overdone it and you're going out of your mind!" I put my hand over my mouth to prevent the strange words from coming out—but the pressure inside my chest increased.

I did not trust myself to speak audibly, but in my mind I said, "God, if this thing inside me doesn't come from You, please take it away..." I waited a few moments, but the voice was still there. "God, if it's You who is giving me these words," I continued, "help me not to be afraid! Help me to accept them!" I moved my hand from my mouth.

Immediately the strange words that I had heard inside my chest began to flow out through my lips, and I realized that I myself was actually speaking them. It was hard to believe that it was my own voice I was listening to. What language was I speaking? I had a fair knowledge of both English and German—it was not either of those. How could I articulate so clearly words that I had never heard before? Yet there was a rhythmic beauty about them that sounded almost like poetry.

With the continuing outflow of this new kind of speech, there came a gradual relief from the intense pressure inside me. These words in the unknown language were saying for me whatever it was that I had struggled in vain to express in my own language. The longer the words flowed, the deeper became my sense of release and fulfillment. Like a river in flood sweeping pieces of debris before it, these unknown words were sweeping away the last barriers of fear and self-consciousness.

Eventually the flow of language ceased, and a deep stillness followed. Never in my life had I known such total relaxation. My mind and my body alike were perfectly at rest. My eyes were closed and yet I had no feeling of sleepiness.

After an unmeasured interval of time I became aware of a new sound. It came from somewhere out in front of me, but a considerable distance away. I opened my eyes and sat up in bed to see where the sound was coming from. The next moment I gasped.

The room was no longer dark, and the bedroom wall in front of me had disappeared! I was looking through the space where the wall had been onto an area about sixty-feet square, which appeared to be the top of an immense, uneven rock. Every crack and crevice in the rock's surface was etched in black shadow by the light of a full moon that hung low in the sky behind.

But my eyes were riveted on a woman who stood in the center, swaying with the motions of a slow, sensuous dance and chanting in a shrill, clear voice. She was wearing a long embroidered dress, gathered around her hips with a scarf, and she had an earthen jar balanced on her head. Her hands rested on her hips, and her feet were bare. In a wide circle around the woman, a group of men sat cross-legged on the rock, clapping their hands in time with her song. They were wearing some kind of long, dark tunic, and their heads were covered by flowing white scarves, fastened with plaited cords that gleamed like gold in the moonlight.

To my own surprise, I felt no sense of fear. I was not dreaming—I knew that. I was wide awake, and I was really "there." The scene before me was unlike anything I had ever seen or even heard of. Yet I did not feel a stranger. I was part of it—I "belonged." I tried to catch the words that the woman was singing but I could not. The rhythm of her dance appealed to my own love of dancing. I felt the urge to enter the ring and dance with her.

Suddenly the scene was gone. My room was dark once more. As my eyes adjusted to the change, I could just make out the familiar outlines of my dresser standing in its usual place against the wall. My first reaction was one of disappointment. I wanted to know more about those people there on the moonlit rock. Who were they? What race did they belong to? Why did I feel so close to them?

I had traveled in Scandinavia and Western Europe, but I had never seen people like that. Nor did I recall reading about them in history or geography. They were certainly not European; neither were they Asian or African. In my mind I could still hear the woman's shrill, clear chanting, but the melody of her song did not fit in with any musical scale I was familiar with.

"This certainly has been the strangest night of my life," I said to myself. "I ought to be frightened—and yet—and yet I've never felt a greater peace."

The next morning, as usual, Valborg knocked at my bedroom door with the day's first cup of coffee. I intended to say, "Come in," then realized with a shock that the words I uttered were not Danish. The door opened and Valborg stood there with the coffee in her hand.

"What did you say, Miss?" she asked.

With a conscious effort I formed my reply in Danish in my mind before I spoke again. "Valborg, something very strange happened to me last night." I listened carefully to my own words and was relieved to know that I was once again speaking Danish. Struggling to find the right words, I described what had happened to me, making Valborg promise not to breathe a word to anyone about what she had heard.

Left to myself again, I leaned back on the pillow with a sigh of relief—I could still speak Danish when I wanted to! But then another thought came—perhaps I could no longer speak the unknown language?

"Please God," I said, "let me speak that other language, too! It was so beautiful. I don't want to lose it."

For a moment a little lump of fear formed in my throat. Then the joy surged up from inside and the fear melted away. Quietly, but very clearly, I was speaking the unknown language once more.

As the day wore on, I made another discovery—I didn't need to speak the new language aloud. I could do it just as well under my breath. This left me free to do it anytime I felt like it, without worrying about what Valborg might think. It was like having a whole new dimension added to my life. I no longer had to give up doing other things each time I wanted to pray. I could go about my normal daily activities—preparing my lessons or correcting pupils' papers—and yet inwardly I could be praying at the same time in an unknown language.

When Valborg left in the evening, I made my way to my prayer chair with more than usual eagerness. It seemed natural now to start by praying in the unknown language. After a pause, various people began coming to my mind, and I found myself praying for them without any effort in Danish. Then I realized what had happened—the old struggle to break through the prayer barrier was no longer there! My new way of praying in the unknown language had brought me through the barrier without any effort!

―――――――――

Returning from school one afternoon the next week, I stopped on an impulse at a bookstore and bought myself a slim, pocket New Testament. "From now on I'll always have this with me," I said to myself as I slipped it into my purse. My new experience had intensified my desire to study the Scriptures for myself.

One evening at supper later that week I could see that Valborg had something on her mind. "You remember what you told me the other morning, Miss," she said, "about praying and speaking a language that you didn't understand?"

"What about it, Valborg?"

"Well, there are people here in Korsør who do the same thing. They call it 'speaking in tongues.' My sister-in-law went to one of their meetings."

I stopped with my spoon halfway to my mouth. Here was news indeed!

"I think they're called 'Pentecostal,'" Valborg continued, "or something like that. They don't go to church; they meet in a man's house. His name is Rasmussen. He used to be a shoemaker, but now he's a pastor."

Pentecostal! My heart sank. All too vividly I recalled the warning of Erna Storm: "They were rolling on the floor and barking like dogs!...They take people out into Store Bælt...and push them under the water." I shuddered inwardly at the thought. And yet I desperately needed to find someone who could help me understand all that had been happening to me.

Suppressing my inner reservations, I asked Valborg if she could arrange for me to meet Mr. Rasmussen "privately, if possible, without going to one of their meetings." A few days later, Valborg brought back a message that the Rasmussens had invited the two of us over for coffee the next Saturday in the evening.

After supper on Saturday, Valborg and I mounted our bicycles and set out for the Rasmussens' home. We passed through the town center and crossed over some railroad tracks into a series of narrow streets with row houses on either side. Finally we turned into a narrow cul-de-sac and stopped outside the last house on the left. In answer to our knock, a short, chubby man came to the door in his shirtsleeves.

"I'm Pastor Rasmussen," he said, extending a hand calloused by many years at a workbench. "Welcome to our home!"

As his hand touched mine, the warmth of his welcome caught me momentarily off my guard, and before I realized it, I had spoken some words in the unknown language. Instantly his smile broadened and the pressure of his handclasp increased. "Come on in!" he said. "We understand all about that! Esther will be happy to meet you."

Before I had time to feel embarrassed, Valborg and I were sitting side by side on the Rasmussens' sofa. The pastor sat on an upright chair by the open fireplace, while his wife rocked gently back and forth in a wooden rocking chair. The furniture was old and worn, but everything was spotlessly clean.

"So God has baptized you in the Holy Spirit," Pastor Rasmussen resumed. "How did it happen?"

"Is that what it is?" I replied. "I knew that something had happened to me, but I didn't know what to call it." I described my experience with the unknown language two weeks earlier.

"Praise the Lord!" Mrs. Rasmussen exclaimed. "God is really beginning to pour out His Spirit here in Korsør."

"You mean that there are other people in Korsør who have had the same kind of experience?" I asked.

"Oh, yes, there are about twenty people who meet in our house every Sunday and study the Bible together," Pastor Rasmussen said. He picked up a worn leather Bible from the mantelpiece. "You see, the very thing that happened to you is described in here... Here it is in Acts." He placed a stubby finger on the page: "And they were all filled with the Holy Ghost, and began to speak with other tongues, as the Spirit gave them utterance" [Acts 2:4].

"You really believe that's what happened to me?"

"Certainly it is," the pastor answered. "God filled you with His Holy Spirit and gave you a new tongue to pray and to worship with."

"A new tongue... But why do I need another language besides Danish?"

Pastor Rasmussen began to turn the pages of the Bible once more. "Paul explains that in First Corinthians, chapter fourteen... Here, at the beginning, he says that when a person speaks in an unknown tongue, he is speaking mysteries—things too deep for his mind to understand. And then a little further on he says that when you pray in an unknown tongue, it's not your mind that's praying, but your spirit." [See verses 2, 14.]

"Pastor, are you telling me that there's something in me deeper than my mind—something that needs to speak directly to God, without going through the bottleneck of my mind?"

"That's right, Sister Christensen, that's it exactly!" Pastor Rasmussen banged the Bible excitedly on his lap. "It's your spirit—not your mind—that was created for direct personal communion with God, and it can never be fully satisfied with anything less."

For a moment the pastor's enthusiasm disturbed me. Besides, no one had ever addressed me as "sister" before! But, as I thought back over my past life, his explanation made sense. For years I had cultivated my mind—with study and travel, with literature and art and philosophy—and yet there was always something missing, some part of me that was never satisfied. Could that be what the pastor called my "spirit"? And that strange new joy that kept bubbling up inside me—did that come from my spirit rather than my mind?

Mrs. Rasmussen brought the coffee from the kitchen while her husband went on with his explanation. "Here's another verse that explains what God is doing today: 'And it shall come to pass in the last days, saith God, I will pour out of my Spirit upon all flesh: and your sons and your daughters shall prophesy, and your young men shall see visions'" [Acts 2:17].

"Visions!" I exclaimed involuntarily. My mind went to the woman dancing on the rock. "I think that must be..." I checked myself. I had told these people too much about myself already!

Fortunately, Pastor Rasmussen did not seem to notice my interruption. For the next two hours he continued turning the pages of his Bible, from the New Testament to the Old and back again to the New. He treated the whole Bible like the day's newspaper—as if it had just been printed that day. He explained things that I had never heard mentioned in all the hours I had spent in church. I kept wondering how a shoemaker could have learned so much about the Bible.

The next morning, reading the Sunday newspaper, I came across an article in the church section entitled "Who Is the Holy Spirit?" The author, Johannes Neergaard, was the pastor of a Lutheran church in Copenhagen with a national reputation for scholarship. On the spur of the moment I sat down and wrote to him, asking for a personal interview. Rather to my surprise, I received an answer by return mail, offering me an appointment at 2:00 PM the next Friday, February 25.

On Friday I caught a train to Copenhagen—a distance of about sixty miles—and took a taxi direct to the church. A secretary showed me into Pastor Neergaard's study. The pastor was a rather heavy man in his late fifties. His formal black suit was relieved by a white clerical collar and by his silvery gray hair. Two walls of the study were lined with shelves of books from floor to ceiling.

"Pastor," I began, "something has happened to me that I don't understand."

"Something has happened to you, little miss?" Apparently he took me to be considerably younger than I was. There was fatherly concern in his voice. "Are you in any kind of trouble?"

"Oh, no," I answered quickly. "It's nothing like that. You see, I was praying in bed one night and I felt such wonderful joy. And then—well, this other voice came up inside me, and I started to speak—words I didn't understand—still praying to God, that is, but not understanding what I was saying."

I paused and waited anxiously for the pastor's reaction. To my surprise he was not at all taken aback. "Ah, now I understand you," he said. "It sounds to me as though you have been baptized with the Holy Spirit. But that's nothing to be afraid of. My wife and I have both received the same experience. Of course, these things are strange to our good church members, so we have to be careful what we say in our public services."

I breathed a sigh of relief. Pastor Neergaard was saying exactly the same thing as Pastor Rasmussen. But it was much easier for me to identify with Pastor Neergaard. His background was more like my own. I did not need to feel isolated or eccentric, after all.

"But now, little miss," Pastor Neergaard continued, "I want to warn you." He wagged his finger at me in a fatherly way. "Be very careful about all that water splashing."

For a moment I could not follow him. Then I recalled the words of Erna Storm, "They take people out into Store Bælt...."

"Water splashing, Pastor?" I said. "Do you mean taking people out into the water—and—and baptizing them?"

"Not baptizing them, little miss, but *re*baptizing them." The pastor placed the emphasis upon the "re." He went on to explain that there were certain groups, "Splinter groups, you understand," who were actually taking Lutheran church members and forcing them to be immersed in water. "As if one baptism wasn't enough!"

At this point something quite unexpected happened to me. Without any mental effort on my part, words of Scripture that I had read in the last two months began to flash across my mind—phrases, sentences, whole passages having to do with baptism—although I had made no conscious effort to study them, much less to memorize them.

"But, Pastor, doesn't the New Testament tell us that the people who were baptized all went down into the water?" I asked. "Why would people do that just to have a few drops sprinkled on their foreheads?"

"You are speaking about the first century of our era," Pastor Neergaard replied. "But eighteen centuries have passed since then." And he began to outline the various developments of doctrine down the centuries, explaining how these had been embodied in the traditions of the church. "Should we now set aside the wisdom and experience of eighteen centuries?" he concluded.

"But, Pastor, suppose our traditions are not in line with Scripture? Didn't Jesus tell the religious leaders of His day that by their traditions they had made God's Word of no effect? He Himself was the one who said, 'He that believeth and is baptized shall be saved' [Mark 16:16]. Wouldn't that mean that we have to *believe* first—and then be baptized?"

I was amazed at my own boldness, and I could see that Pastor Neergaard was getting upset. His tone was no longer altogether fatherly. "Young lady," he said, "for every Lutheran these questions have been settled once and for all. Your baptism as an infant was effective through the faith of your parents, and then at confirmation you sealed it by your own faith."

The faith of my parents? My own faith? I was certainly not qualified to argue with an eminent theologian, but his words started a whole train of questions in my own mind. How much faith did my parents really have when I was baptized? If so much depended on their faith, it was important for me to know that. More important still, how much faith did I myself have when I was confirmed? I had done it mainly to please my family and the church. Had I ever known what real faith was before the last few weeks?

Eventually the pastor escorted me out onto the steps of the church and there gave me one final piece of counsel: "Let me urge you not to be too hasty in what you say or do. No doubt, many of our church members do not have the faith that they should, but we have to be patient and trust that they will gradually see more of the truth. After all, Rome wasn't built in a day!"

In the train back to Korsør, alone in a first-class compartment, I began to reproach myself. Had I been guilty of arrogance, even of irreverence, in questioning the traditions of the church? Who was I to do that? After all, Pastor Neergaard was a nationally recognized theologian. I myself was amazed at the arguments I had brought forward. Where had they come from? I had never spoken to anyone like that before in my life.

And yet I could not now escape from the logic of my own arguments. The questions I had raised demanded an answer—if not from the pastor, then from myself. What did the New Testament really teach about baptism? I recalled some words of Paul that had made a deep impression on me a few days previously. Pulling out my pocket New Testament, I turned its pages until I found the verses I was looking for:

> How shall we, that are dead to sin, live any longer therein? Know ye not, that so many of us as were baptized into Jesus Christ were baptized into his death? Therefore we are buried with him by baptism into death: that like as Christ was raised up from the dead by the glory of the Father, even so we also should walk in newness of life.
>
> (Romans 6:2–4)

I read these verses over several times. Three experiences stood out clearly—death, burial, resurrection—three successive steps in our identification with Christ. I began to measure my own experience by this standard. I looked back over the life that I had lived up to the last few weeks. Had there ever been anything in all those years that I could truly call a "death to sin" followed by a burial and a resurrection? By no stretch of imagination could I make those words apply to anything that had happened in my infancy or my teens—or at any time since.

Logic was leading me to a conclusion that I was reluctant to accept. Baptism was a burial of the old way of life and a resurrection to a new way of life. That I could see. Equally clearly I could see that I myself had never experienced either a burial or a resurrection such as this. Therefore—what? There was only one possible conclusion: *I had never been baptized.*

I repeated slowly to myself the words of Jesus that I had already quoted to Pastor Neergaard: "He that believeth and is baptized shall be saved" (Mark 16:16). I knew beyond a doubt that I now *believed.* What was left but to be baptized? In my apartment, the day that Jesus appeared to me, I had promised God, "If You will show me Jesus as a living reality, I will follow Him." God had answered my prayer. I dared not now go back on my promise.

To whom could I go for baptism? I knew of only one person, Pastor Rasmussen. But suppose people in Korsør found out! News traveled fast in such a small, gossipy community. It was not difficult for me to imagine what might follow.

Denmark was possibly the most totally Lutheran nation on earth. The Lutheran Church was the state church of the nation. Out of four million Danes, over 90 percent were members of it. In matters of religion, the school where I taught, like all state schools, was under the jurisdiction of the church.

How would the ecclesiastical authorities react to a teacher being baptized by a Pentecostal pastor?

And what about my fellow teachers? In a town such as Korsør we teachers were a small, privileged group, looked up to by the rest of the community. For me to be associated—even by the one act of baptism—with the despised Pentecostals would be viewed by my colleagues as a betrayal of the social and intellectual standards of our profession. I already knew how Erna Storm would react. But what about Soren? And others of my colleagues whose respect and friendship I cherished?

What was I to do? In a silent prayer I breathed the words that I had read so many times of late: "Teach me thy way, O Lord." (See Psalm 25:4.) Then I glanced out the window. The train was nearing Korsør. As it jarred to a standstill, I knew that I had already made my decision: *I would go straight to Pastor Rasmussen and ask him to baptize me.*

I collected my bicycle from the station yard and set out directly for the home of the Rasmussens. All the way my fears followed me. You'll lose Soren. You'll lose your job. You'll throw away everything you've worked for all these years.

And then some words came to me from an unexpected source—one of the history textbooks that we used at school. Ironically enough, they were the words of Luther himself as he answered the religious court that had arraigned him: "Here I stand, bound in my conscience. I can do no other." I, too, had come to a place where I had to answer my own conscience.

The Rasmussens were obviously surprised to see me, but their welcome was warm. "Pastor Rasmussen," I said, "I want to be baptized—really baptized. Would you do it for me?"

"Well," he said, "we're building a meeting place with a baptistry, and as soon as it's ready we're planning a baptismal service. We can put your name down to be baptized then."

"But by that time I may not have the courage," I told him. "The longer I wait, the harder it will be."

Pastor Rasmussen rubbed his chin thoughtfully. "In the summer we sometimes baptize people in Store Bælt, but at this time of year that wouldn't be possible." He paused for a moment, then turned to his wife. "Could we borrow a bathtub, Esther, and put it in the kitchen?"

"Why not?" Mrs. Rasmussen replied. "I'm sure Mrs. Svenson would let us use hers."

"How would that do?" Pastor Rasmussen turned back to me. "Would you be willing to be baptized in our kitchen—in a bathtub?"

"I don't care where you do it," I replied, "as long as my old life is really buried!"

"Let's see," Pastor Rasmussen went on. "Today is Friday. Come back tomorrow evening at about six, and we'll have the tub out in the kitchen waiting for you."

The next evening I duly presented myself at the Rasmussens' home. Mrs. Rasmussen helped me to put on a long white nightgown and led me into the kitchen. In the center of the stone floor stood a large zinc bathtub filled with water. "We've taken the chill off the water for you," she assured me.

A few of the local fishermen's wives were there to witness the ceremony. With a shock I recognized one of them as the mother of one of my pupils. Up to that moment I had secretly been hoping that what I was doing would not have to be made public. Now I knew that within a few days it would be broadcast to the whole school, teachers and pupils alike.

My eyes took in the details of the scene. The bare shelves and counters were scrupulously clean, but worn with many years of scrubbing. Two large black frying pans were suspended on nails above the stove, where a kettle still simmered gently. The only ornament was a wooden breadboard, hanging on one wall. On it were painted the words, "Give us this day our daily bread."

I could feel my bare feet becoming numb with the cold from the uncarpeted stone floor. It would have been impossible to imagine a scene that contrasted more sharply with all that I was used to. No one but God Himself could have made the breach so total. By that one symbolic act I was renouncing my whole inheritance—social, cultural, intellectual, and religious.

Once more I weighed the consequences of what I was about to do. Was I really willing to forego the acceptance of those whom I had known all my life—to be an alien among my own people from that moment on—forever? Yet this was what I myself had asked for—to be "buried." How much from the past life could a person take with him to the grave? Only now did I understand just how like a burial it would actually feel.

The ceremony itself was brief and simple. We stood around the kitchen in a circle facing each other. Pastor Rasmussen read some words of Jesus from Matthew:

> If any man will come after me, let him deny himself, and take up his cross, and follow me. For whosoever will save his life shall lose it: and whosoever will lose his life for my sake shall find it.
>
> (Matthew 16:24–25)

Closing his Bible, Pastor Rasmussen offered a prayer, but my mind was unable to follow him. I was taken up with the words of Jesus that he had just read: *Whosoever will lose his life...shall find it.* I saw that my baptism that night was the first part of an exchange. I was *losing* my life, as I had known it up to then. In return, there would be another life opened up to me that I would have to *find*.

When Pastor Rasmussen concluded his prayer, I took my place in the bathtub in a sitting posture. "Upon confession of your faith," I heard him say, "I baptize you into the death and resurrection of Christ. In the name of the Father, and of the Son, and of the Holy Ghost. Amen!" Then he pressed me gently but firmly backward beneath the surface of the water, held me there a moment, and brought me up again.

As I sat in the bathtub, with the water running down my face, I was no longer conscious of my surroundings. Only one thing mattered at that moment—my fears and struggles were at an end! In their place a deep, settled peace filled my heart. This was God's own testimony of His approval upon my act. In the days that lay ahead I could hold on to that assurance. *I had done what God had required of me.*

5

DR. KARLSSON'S MESSAGE

By the middle of the next week the news of my baptism had reached the entire school. The reaction of the pupils was more open and more immediate than that of the teachers. Walking across the schoolyard, I would be greeted by shrill cries of "Hallelujah!" Approaching my classroom, I would hear the sounds of animated discussion. As I entered, this would die down to an unnatural silence, broken only by a few furtive giggles. One day I found the letters H-A-L-L-E-L-U-J-A-H scrawled in a childish hand across the full width of my blackboard.

The conduct of my fellow teachers was less overt, but more wounding. I soon realized that they no longer wished to be seen walking with me across the schoolyard. They would either hurry across ahead of me, pretending that they had not seen me, or else they would find some pretext to linger around or turn in some other direction, until I had gone over by myself. When I entered the teachers' common room, a sudden silence would fall. Then everyone would start talking rather loudly about trivial matters.

One afternoon after my last class I found Soren waiting for me in the corridor. "Do you have a moment?" he asked.

"Of course," I replied. "We haven't seen much of each other lately." We fell into step and started walking slowly toward the schoolyard.

"Do you mind if I ask you a frank question?" Soren paused, and seeing that I raised no objection, he continued, "All this business about—" he hesitated, then forced himself to utter the word—"*baptism*. Is this all a part of the search for truth?"

"I suppose you could call it that. You see, when you seek for the truth, and you believe you've found it—well, then you're faced with the challenge of obeying it!"

"To find the truth...? Isn't that what every religious group claims to have done?" And when I did not answer: "You know Erna Storm is getting up a petition requesting your resignation as a teacher?"

By this time we had reached the edge of the schoolyard. I paused momentarily, to give Soren an opportunity to go on ahead of me. To his credit, however, he was willing to run the gauntlet with me. When we were halfway across, there came the usual, shrill *Hallelujahs*.

"Doesn't that disturb you?" Soren asked.

"Well, I can't say that I enjoy it," I answered, "but it's a small price to pay for what I've found."

"What is that, Lydia?"

"Happiness, Soren, real happiness deep inside me, in spite of anything that people say or do. I feel like the merchant in Christ's parable who found one pearl so valuable that he sold all he had to buy it." ("Perhaps even our chances of happiness together," I added to myself, as Soren's troubled, questioning gaze met mine.)

I still awaited the official reaction of the ecclesiastical authorities. It was not long in coming. On March 9, I was summoned to the office of the Lutheran pastor who was responsible for all matters of religion within the school. He asked me to explain my action in being baptized, which I did as best I could.

From there my case was referred to the higher ecclesiastical authority known as the provost. In due course I was summoned to the office of the provost in the neighboring town of Slagelse, and once again made to account for my behavior.

The provost clearly regarded me as one of his sheep that had strayed. "Why did you not come to me first," he asked, "before you did a thing like this?"

"Provost," I answered, "I attended church for years, but I always came out feeling more confused than when I went in. In the end I felt there was no one to turn to but God Himself."

"Doesn't every generation think it has a monopoly on the truth?" the provost sighed. "I shouldn't be surprised if you also think you have a missionary calling. I thought that myself when I was your age."

"But, Provost, perhaps you really did have a—" I stopped at the look in the provost's eyes. Was it anger? Or was it anguish? A rebuke—or a plea? Either way, I knew I had said too much.

For several days I could not forget what I had seen in the provost's eyes. Here was a man successful in his profession and respected in the community, conscientiously seeking to serve God and his fellowman. And yet—his troubled gaze reminded me of Soren. Was there something more in life that even the provost had not found—perhaps the one thing that mattered most? Why should he speak about a missionary calling? I did not understand what that meant, and yet I could not dismiss the phrase from my mind.

Meanwhile, my story was taken up by the newspapers, locally first, then nationwide. Returning from school one afternoon I found on my table a copy of *Morning*, Denmark's most widely circulated national paper.

"I brought that paper for you to see, Miss," Valborg said. "There's an article about you inside—right on the center page."

Sure enough, a headline extended the full width of the page: CAN A TONGUES SPEAKER REMAIN AS A TEACHER IN A STATE SCHOOL? The writer made much of my association with the Pentecostals, whom he dismissed as "a sect of recent origin, without formal education or theology." However, his attitude toward my case was not altogether unfavorable. He raised the question of how far the Lutheran Church had the right to dictate the personal religious beliefs of teachers in state schools.

"It must be terrible," said Valborg, "to know that everybody's talking about you like that right across the country."

"In a way that's true, Valborg," I replied, "and yet it's helped me to understand a verse that puzzled me when I first read it: *'Blessed are they which are persecuted for righteousness' sake.'* At the time I couldn't understand how anybody could be blessed by a thing like that. But in the midst of all the criticism and the opposition, I've had a joy and a peace I never knew before."

After that, each time I was referred to in a newspaper, Valborg supplied me with a copy and studied me anxiously to see my reaction. For the next few weeks my case was debated at length in the press. Prominent national personalities argued both for and against me. However, there seemed to be a general opinion that teachers in state schools should be permitted greater individual freedom in their religious opinions.

Early in April, Mr. Pedersen, the principal of the school, sent for me. It was mainly his recommendation that had obtained for me my post as director of domestic science, and I knew that he was pleased with the way I had run my department.

"Miss Christensen," he said, "I have to inform you that your case has been referred to the Ministry of Education in Copenhagen, and they are going to discuss it in the parliament. Once it gets there, no one knows how long they may take to reach a decision. However, I will keep you informed of developments." Then he added in a more personal way, "I'm sure everything's going to turn out all right."

I thanked him but wondered inwardly what the grounds for his confidence were.

By this time the Pentecostal people had completed their meeting place, and it seemed right for me to begin attending their services. The Rasmussens did their best to make me welcome, but from the members of their congregation I did not feel the acceptance for which I had hoped. No matter how hard I tried to adjust, I was still "different."

All the women wore clothes that were plain to the point of being dowdy. When attending their meetings, I put on my least elegant dresses. But that was not enough. All Christians, it seemed, wore dark stockings. Mine were too light in color. Reluctantly I bought two pairs of ugly black ones.

My language also caused a problem. I was too "educated." Education was "worldly." The difference in my intellectual and social background meant more to them than it did to me. The first few times I prayed aloud in a meeting, a kind of disapproving silence fell on the rest of those present.

Back home in my apartment after one such meeting, I took stock of my position. My fellow teachers no longer wished to associate with me. The Lutheran Church regarded me as an apostate from the faith. The Pentecostals were reluctant to accept me as one of them. The nation at large was discussing my case, and the parliament was to decide on my future as a teacher. It was hard to understand how all this had developed out of my simple, personal discovery that Christ was alive and the Bible was true.

Shortly before Easter I received a brief, but agonized, letter from Mother: "All our friends are talking about you....Our priest came to see me....I don't understand why you would do a thing like that."

I spent the Easter weekend at home with Mother, sharing with her all that had been happening to me. "You know I haven't studied these things myself," she said eventually. "All I want is to be sure that you haven't done something bad."

"Mother," I assured her, "this is the best thing that ever happened in my life!"

———————

Near the end of June I was summoned once again to Mr. Pedersen's office. As soon as I entered, he stood up and held out a letter for me to see. "This is the answer from the Ministry of Education about your case."

I felt my heart beginning to beat faster. I had been praying for God's will to be done, but now that the moment had come, I realized how much my position in the school really meant to me.

Mr. Pedersen continued, "The Minister of Education has granted permission for you to remain as a teacher—if you agree to sign this statement." He handed me a sheet of paper, with the official heading of the Ministry of Education.

I read the statement through carefully. Then, without a further word, I picked up the pen from Mr. Pedersen's desk and signed the statement.

"Wait a minute!" he protested. "Don't be so hasty! You've waited months for this decision, and now you sign it without knowing what it says."

"Oh, no," I answered him, "I've seen what it says. It says that I will undertake not to influence the children with regard to the baptism of infants. If I wanted to tell the children anything, it would not be about the baptism of infants, but about the baptism of believers."

Mr. Pedersen looked relieved. "You know, Miss Christensen," he said, "I've never studied that question, but I've noticed something new about you these last months—a kind of contentment, should I say? Tell me, is it wrong to be envious?"

———————

Outwardly my position as a teacher at the school was once again assured. I had openly challenged both the authority and the theology of the state

church, and the national parliament had, in effect, upheld me. Inwardly, however, a change had taken place in me that was not affected by the parliament's
decision. Through the act of baptism I had lost my old life. There was a finality
about this that could not be changed. It seemed that I must now begin to plan
a new life to take the place of the old one. Yet I had no idea how to set about
this.

From the Rasmussens I heard about some large Pentecostal churches in
Sweden to which people from other European countries frequently went for
spiritual counsel. Perhaps that was the source from which I should seek help.
I decided to use my summer vacation for this purpose.

I crossed over to the south of Sweden at the beginning of August and
journeyed northward by stages to Stockholm, visiting Pentecostal churches
in various cities on the way. Fortunately there was no language barrier. The
Danish and Swedish languages are close enough to each other so that a Dane
and a Swede can carry on a conversation together, each speaking his own language, but understanding the language of the other.

I reached Stockholm by about the middle of August and registered at
a hotel near the center of the city. Looking down from my window at noon
one day on the busy intersection below, I became absorbed in the streams
of people and traffic flowing ceaselessly in every direction. "So many people
going in so many directions," I thought to myself, "Does it make no difference
in which direction a person goes? Or is there only one way that is the right way
for each person?"

On Sunday morning I attended Stockholm's largest Pentecostal church.
The worship of the great congregation was inspiring and the sermon was clear
and forceful, but it did not offer me any answer to my personal search. It was
announced that the preacher in the evening would be a missionary from the
Congo named Bengt Karlsson.

I returned for the evening service with a sense of frustration. I had spent
three weeks in Sweden, attending half a dozen churches, and I was due to start
on my journey back to Denmark the next day. Yet I was no nearer to finding
what I had come to Sweden to seek, and I could not see how a talk on mission
work in the Congo would help me.

For his opening text Bengt Karlsson quoted a passage from the apostle
Paul: "For we are his workmanship, created in Christ Jesus unto good works,

which God hath before ordained that we should walk in them" (Ephesians 2:10). He applied this to his own life, describing the steps that had taken him from a successful medical practice in southern Sweden to an area of primitive jungle in the Congo.

But I no longer heard him. The scene in the church faded from my view. The last words of the opening text echoed and reechoed through my mind: "good works, which God hath before ordained that we should walk in them." Gradually their meaning became plain: *God has already assigned to each one of us a special task in life.*

Here was the answer to my question! I did not have to plan the work that I would do in life. I had to find the work that God had already planned for me. There was a special task appointed for me by God, which could not be carried out by any other person in the world. My supreme responsibility in life was to find and to fulfill that task. If I did not carry out my task, it would be left undone. No one else could take my place.

The air in the church was warm—almost close. Yet I began to tremble in my seat. The sense of my personal responsibility was awesome. In eternity I would have to answer for that moment. I was accountable to God for what I did with my life! With my head bowed and my eyes closed, I breathed a prayer: "Lord, show me the work that You have assigned to me, and I will do my best to carry it out."

The scene in the church came back into focus. Dr. Karlsson was explaining his plans to construct a small hospital in the heart of the jungle. The equipment would have to be imported from Sweden; labor and building materials would be supplied by his own African congregation. By strict economy and careful planning the total cost could be kept below four thousand dollars. "We are asking God's people to help us with this task," Dr. Karlsson concluded.

"You have money to help him!" I turned to see if someone had spoken to me from behind, but the people there were getting out their hymnbooks. Yet the words were as clear as if they had been spoken audibly.

The morning I had left Korsør for Sweden, I had received a statement from the savings bank. The balance standing to my credit was 12,212.25 Danish kroner—something over $3,000. This represented the amount left from my father's legacy—in 1927 a substantial sum.

At the close of the service I introduced myself to Dr. Karlsson and asked if I could speak with him privately. A few minutes later I found myself seated with him and his wife at a kitchen table in a small apartment behind the church.

"Dr. Karlsson," I began, "I've only recently come into this new life and there are still many things I don't understand. But at the end of your talk tonight I believe I heard God speak to me, telling me to give you three thousand dollars for your hospital."

I could see that the Karlssons were taken aback by the amount that I had named. "Sister Christensen," the doctor said, "before you commit yourself to such a large sum, I would ask you to pray carefully and make absolutely sure it was God's voice you heard."

I thanked him for his words of caution, but inwardly I was sure already.

"Please tell us how you came into this new life in the Holy Spirit," Mrs. Karlsson said.

I began to describe my search for the true purpose of life, and the strange experiences that followed. The Karlssons were such sympathetic listeners that I felt no embarrassment. I even told them about the woman I had seen dancing, with the men sitting cross-legged around her. "I don't know if there really is some country where the people do dress like that," I added.

Dr. Karlsson smiled. "Perhaps I can answer that question for you," he said. "On our way back from the Congo this spring we made a special trip to the Holy Land. The style of dress there, both for men and for women, is exactly as you described it."

"The Holy Land..." I began. Why had I never thought of that? And why should I feel that sudden surge of excitement? I remembered how I had longed to know more about those people in my vision.

"Let me ask you to do one thing, Sister Christensen—pray earnestly that you may find and do God's will for your life," Dr. Karlsson resumed with a gentle urgency in his voice. "That is the purpose for which we were created from eternity, and in the long run nothing else can truly satisfy us. I've proved that in my own experience."

For the next hour Dr. Karlsson related the story of his own search for fulfillment—the surrender of a lifetime ambition, the loneliness and hardship of the African jungle, the heartbreaking struggle with disease and superstition. "And yet," he concluded, "if I had to make my choice all over again, I wouldn't ask for anything else. I've found life's highest satisfaction."

Early the next morning I started on the long journey back to Denmark. I needed the time to meditate on what had happened the night before. Had I been hasty to promise such a large sum of money for a hospital in a place I had never heard of? I could have lived comfortably for at least two years on that amount. Or was this the kind of treasure that Jesus warned us not to lay up on earth? After all, my salary as a teacher was now secure again.

More important than the money I had promised to give was the new direction that I had received for my future. I reminded myself of what God had shown me. I did not need to make a plan of my own for my life. God had a plan already made. All I needed to do was find it.

I reached Korsør late that night. Early the next day I withdrew the entire balance from my savings account and sent it by registered mail to Dr. Karlsson in Stockholm. I had half expected an inward struggle, but the opposite was the case. When I handed the letter to the clerk in the post office, I felt as if a burden had been lifted from my back. I was free to devote myself to the task that I now knew lay before me—that of discovering God's plan for my life.

———————

School reopened at the end of August. My domestic-science department was running more smoothly than ever, and Mr. Pedersen went out of his way to show his appreciation. But, as the term wore on, I found myself struggling with a strange, inner restlessness. The words of Dr. Karlsson's text kept coming back to me. My work in school was a "good work"—but was it the work that God had actually ordained for me? There were other teachers in Denmark just as well qualified to teach domestic science. Was there some other, special work waiting for me—some task that would never be fulfilled unless I would take it up?

Dr. Karlsson had suggested that the people I had seen in my vision might be from the Holy Land. Almost against my will, I began to turn my attention in that direction. Apart from the Karlssons, I had never met anyone who had actually been there. This ten-thousand-square-mile area of land at the meeting point of three continents—Europe, Asia, and Africa—had played a strangely significant role in human history, yet for the long period from the close of the Bible record to our time reliable information was hard to obtain. I visited libraries, secondhand bookstores, even newspaper morgues. Eventually I put together for myself an outline of the land's history.

Originally known as the land of Canaan, it had been promised by God as an inheritance successively to the three Hebrew patriarchs: Abraham, Isaac, and Jacob (renamed Israel). Later, under David and Solomon, Jacob's descendants—known collectively as Israel—had established a powerful and prosperous empire, with Jerusalem as its magnificent capital. Then religious and political decline set in, and in the following centuries the land was subjugated in turn by various rival empires: Babylon, Persia, Greece, and Rome. Rising in revolt against Rome, the Jewish nation was finally defeated with fearful cruelty. Jerusalem with its sacred temple was destroyed, and the survivors were scattered among the surrounding nations, to begin a period of exile that was to last for more than eighteen centuries. Their place was taken by Gentiles from bordering countries.

In the seventh century of our era, the Holy Land fell to the conquering armies of the Arabs, devout followers of the new Islamic religion founded by Mohammed. For the next thirteen centuries—except for a brief period under the Crusaders in the eleventh century—the land was conquered and ruled by a succession of Muslim peoples, culminating in four hundred years under the Ottoman Turks. This long series of conquests, coupled with increasing neglect, eventually reduced much of the area to a wasteland, stripped of trees, with cities crumbling into decay and malarial swamps covering once-fertile fields.

Finally, ten years previously, at the end of the World War of 1914–1918, the feudal dominion of the Turks had given way to a British Mandate over two adjacent territories divided by the Jordan river—Palestine to the west, Transjordan to the east. This change, however, had only provoked new tensions and problems. The technology of the twentieth century was beginning to invade customs and ways of life that extended back, almost unchanged, to the time of Abraham. Arab peasants, whose families had tilled the same small acreages for a thousand years or more, were suddenly confronted by the pressure of land-hungry Jewish immigrants, backed by modern skills and equipment and by the financial resources of international Zionism.

Behind the scenes, the great powers were vying with one another for the control of strategic areas of the Middle East, such as the Suez Canal, and the world's richest oil supplies. The British administration was juggling desperately with the rival claims of various racial, political, and religious groups, but reaching no lasting resolution. I found the situation bluntly summed up by a Danish journalist who had recently returned from the area: "The question is not whether open conflict will break out, but only how soon."

There was nothing appealing about the picture of the Holy Land that I had thus formed. I tried to dismiss it from my mind, but I could not. Was this perhaps a further indication that God's purpose for my life was somehow connected with that land and its people? I knew of only one way to seek an answer—by prayer. It was hard to begin praying for an area so alien and so remote, but I had committed myself to seeking God's purpose, and I had to follow the only way that seemed open to me.

In the weeks that followed I spent many wearisome hours kneeling at my green armchair. Often I was tempted to give up. Why pray for something so distant and unreal? Slowly I began to realize that God was teaching me to rely upon the Holy Spirit. Whenever I felt in need of special encouragement, I would turn to the words of Paul: "Likewise the Spirit also helpeth our infirmities: for we know not what we should pray for as we ought: but the Spirit itself maketh intercession for us" (Romans 8:26).

When I could make no progress by praying in my own language, I would yield to the Holy Spirit and let Him pray through me in a language of His own choosing. By this time I had discovered that God had given me not merely one new language, but several. There was one that was soft and fluent, rather like Italian. This was the first language I had received—the night I had the vision of the woman dancing. There was another that contained many gutturals—more like Dutch. A third had a nasal twang unlike any language I had ever heard spoken. There were still others that were not so easy to identify. It seemed that a particular language was appropriate to a certain theme of prayer, or to a certain mood of my own spirit.

Sometimes, after praying for a while in an unknown language, I would change over to Danish, only to be surprised at the things I heard myself praying for. I realized that prayer of this kind, even in Danish, was being given to me directly by the Holy Spirit. In such a case, praying in an unknown language served as a stairway leading me upward to a higher level of prayer than my own mind was capable of—although I might later change back to Danish.

As I continued praying regularly in this way through October and November, I became aware that my inner attitudes were undergoing a profound change. Was it actually possible to love people whom I had never seen? I knew well what it was to love my parents and my sisters. Now I began to feel that I had another *family* in the land that I was praying for—a family whom I had never seen and whose names I did not know. Yet love for them was flowing out through my prayers. The more I prayed, the stronger my love became.

Pastor Rasmussen invited me to attend a special day of prayer in his church on Sunday, December 4, 1927. About thirty of us came together in the morning and spent the first part of the day alternately singing, praying, and reading from the Scriptures. Early in the afternoon an unusual stillness came down upon us all. For a period of five or ten minutes no one attempted to pray aloud. Our communion with God and with each other had become so close that it no longer needed to be expressed in audible words.

Kneeling in my place I felt a sense of God's presence overshadowing me. It seemed to be coming down over me like dew falling in the silence of the night. My heart beat faster with anticipation. After a while the face of a baby girl appeared before me. She was looking up at me from some kind of a box, but the details were not clear. It was her black, solemn eyes that held my attention. I longed to communicate with her—but I could not!

For several days afterward, each time I closed my eyes in prayer, I would see the child's face gazing up at me. Was she a part of my unseen family?

Over the Christmas holidays I went back to Brønderslev for our traditional family reunion. Outwardly nothing had changed, but I was no longer a part of it all. A gulf had come between my real family and me. Somehow I began to feel closer to my unseen family in that distant land.

I was back again in Korsør for New Year's Day, 1928. It had been just a year since Jesus had appeared to me there in my apartment. Two months later I had been baptized. Who could have foreseen all the changes that would follow?

And more, I felt, still lay ahead. My impression became stronger and stronger that God was directing me to the Holy Land. Could I ask Him to show me more than this—the very place I was to go, the kind of work I was to do?

As I prayed along this line, I was reminded of a game that I had often played in childhood. One person would go out of the room, and in his absence the other people would conceal a ring somewhere in the room. Then the person would be allowed back. As he moved near the place where the ring was hidden, the others would say, "Now you're getting warm!" If he moved in the wrong direction, they would say, "Now you're getting cold!" When he came really close, they would tell him, "Now you're hot!"

Each time I prayed for the Holy Land and its people, there was a warmth in my spirit that showed me I was moving in the right direction. One day I felt strongly prompted to pray for the city of Jerusalem. Immediately the warmth intensified. Was this the Holy Spirit's way of telling me, "Now you're hot!"? Each day for a week my prayers followed the same pattern, and each time there came the same reaction. Was Jerusalem the place?

But why Jerusalem? I knew no one there and had no contacts of any kind. What would I do? I tried to picture myself in various situations—but I did not seem to fit in any. I told myself that it was absurd to consider such a thing, but in spite of all my arguments I could not fight off the conviction: *God was asking me to go to Jerusalem*, even if I did not know why or what I was to do.

Innumerable questions began to assail my mind. What about money, for instance? I had given the last of my father's legacy to Dr. Karlsson. If I resigned my position as a teacher, I would lose my salary from the school. Because of the nationwide publicity given to my baptism in water and in the Holy Spirit, I was sure that no recognized missionary society in Denmark would accept me as a candidate. The Pentecostal people had no money to spare. In fact, the money I was able to give out of my salary was one main part of the pastor's support.

All my life I had lived in financial abundance. Could I trust God to provide for me in a remote and unfamiliar land without a commitment from any church or missionary society? Hardly anyone would even know that I was there. Could God cause people to send me money, although they did not recognize me as a missionary and did not know what I needed? For a week I argued this question back and forth in my mind. Eventually I decided that I would pray for money right where I was and see what happened.

As long as I still held my well-paid position as a teacher, it would be most unusual for anyone to offer me money. However, I decided to ask God for this very thing. I prayed a simple and specific prayer: "Please, God, I want someone to give me five dollars before midnight tomorrow. If You will do this, then I will know that You can cause people to supply my needs even in Jerusalem."

All the next day at school I was reproaching myself for praying such an absurd prayer and at the same time trying to imagine who could possibly give me five dollars. It would not be one of my colleagues. They all knew how well I was provided for. Perhaps there would be a letter in the mail from some distant relative... In spite of myself, I cycled home much faster than usual.

"Did the postman come today, Valborg?" I asked, as soon as I got inside the door. Valborg handed me a single envelope, postmarked in Fyn. My heart beat a little faster as I opened it. It was a note from one of Kezia's children: "Dear Aunt Lydia, Thank you for the gift you sent for my birthday." But—no money!

By 9:30 PM it was clear that the money was not coming. I did not know whether to feel disappointed or relieved. If the money did not come, it would indicate that God was not asking me to go to Jerusalem. I had been mistaken, after all, about His guidance.

Or did it merely indicate that my prayer had been wrong in the first place? Why should God send me an exact amount on a certain day, when I really did not need the money at all? I should not have prayed such an unreasonable prayer.

I was on my way to bed when there was a knock at the door. My heart was literally pounding as I went to open it. My visitor was Kristine Sonderby, the school librarian who attended the Evangelical Mission by the harbor.

"I hope you won't think this very strange," she began, before I even had time to ask her inside. "But this evening I was saying my prayers, and something happened..." She was fumbling inside her big black purse while she spoke. "I had the strongest impression that God wanted me to bring you this." She drew five dollars out of her purse and handed them to me. After lingering for a few moments in the doorway, she took her leave, obviously embarrassed by her own unconventional behavior.

After Kristine had gone, my knees seemed to buckle under me. I had to sit for several minutes at the dining table, waiting for my strength to return. With less than two hours left in the day, God had sent me exactly the amount that I had asked for. I no longer had any excuse to doubt! God had given me convincing proof that He was able to provide for me in Jerusalem—or anywhere else that He might ask me to go!

The next day, during a break at school, Kristine again came up to me, fumbling in her purse just as she had done the previous evening. "I don't know why I acted the way I did last night," she said. "I really intended to give you twenty dollars all along, but for some reason I only gave you five last night. Here is the other fifteen." She handed me the bills as she spoke.

"Kristine," I said, "you'll probably never know how important this is to me—but I want to thank you for obeying God's voice."

I was aware of her eyes searching me through the thick lenses. "I can see that you really have changed," she said. "You don't even smoke any longer... Could you tell me how it happened?"

As simply as I could, I described how Jesus had revealed Himself to me and then filled me with the Holy Spirit.

"Lydia, I believe it all," Kristine commented at the end. "There's just one thing I don't understand—about speaking in an unknown language. We've always been taught that things like that ceased with the apostles and that it would be wrong for us to expect them today." Did I detect a note of wistfulness in her voice?

"Why don't you pray about that?" I replied. "Ask God to show you the truth direct from the Bible."

"Yes, I think you're right—I'll do that." Kristine squeezed my hand with a warmth I had never seen in her before, and we parted.

I spent the rest of the day meditating on what had happened. God had not merely given me proof that He was able to supply my need in Jerusalem, but He had also taught me two important lessons about prayer.

First, I must not try to work out in advance how God would answer my prayer. It was God's responsibility, not mine, to decide how the answer would come. I had ruled out the possibility of the money coming from any of my fellow teachers, but God had chosen to send it by Kristine.

Second, God was willing to give more than I had faith to pray for. Because I had specifically asked for five dollars, God had caused Kristine to bring me exactly that amount the first time. However, He had actually put it in her heart to give me four times as much. I must not limit God by asking for too little!

In Korsør, winter was beginning to yield to spring. The early gleams of spring sunshine accentuated the white eaves and red roofs of the trim brick houses. I had enjoyed Korsør from the first day that I moved there, but never had it seemed so attractive to me as it did just then. Was God really asking me to exchange all this for a distant, primitive land, where people, customs, and scenery would all be alien and unfamiliar? My commitment to God's purpose would be sealed by a final act—the handing in of my resignation to Mr. Pedersen. Week after week I put this off.

Over the Easter weekend I went to hear a veteran missionary from China, named Arne Konrad, preaching at the Pentecostal church. On the closing Sunday night he spoke on a text from Hebrews: "By faith Abraham, when he was called to go out into a place which he should after receive for an inheritance, obeyed; and he went out, not knowing whither he went" (Hebrews 11:8). Mr. Konrad painted a vivid picture of Abraham leaving the comfort and security of his home in Ur and setting out for a land he knew nothing about, relying solely on God's promise. I felt that every word he spoke was addressed to me personally.

At the end of the service, I asked to speak to Mr. Konrad privately. I described the way that God had been directing me to resign my position and go to Jerusalem and the hesitation I felt about making this final commitment. When I had finished, he looked at me for a few moments with his gray eyes glittering beneath bushy white eyebrows. Finally he said, "Sister Christensen, Denmark is full of spiritual cripples who have heard the call of God but were afraid to step out in faith. Don't you become one of them!"

His words were still ringing in my ears when I got back to my apartment. I went straight over to my desk, wrote out my letter of resignation, and placed it on top of the books that I had put out ready to take to school the next morning.

As I lay waiting for sleep to come, I pictured the finality of the act I was about to make. It was good-bye to my whole familiar world of Korsør, and the first step out into an unknown future—one for which I could make no preparation and no provision. To fight back the doubts and fears that flooded in upon me, I kept repeating the words of Mr. Konrad's text: "By faith Abraham...went out, not knowing whither he went." Finally I fell asleep with those words still on my lips.

At school the next morning I had the second period free. As soon as the bell rang for the close of the first period, I took my letter of resignation to Mr. Pedersen in his office. He welcomed me and gave me a seat.

"Mr. Pedersen," I said, holding out my letter, "I wanted to bring you this in person. It's my letter of resignation."

"Your letter of..." Mr. Pedersen paused with his hand half stretched out to receive the letter. "You mean you're leaving us?"

I related how I had become convinced that God had been speaking to me about going to Jerusalem. At the end Mr. Pedersen stood up, gave me his hand, and wished me Godspeed. "I'm not sure I understand," he added, "but I respect you for being faithful to your convictions."

As I stepped out into the corridor, I almost ran into Soren.

"Good morning," he said. "What takes you into the principal's office at this early hour?"

"I've just handed in my resignation."

"Your resignation! You've never said a word about that!" Soren was visibly shocked. "I do hope it isn't because of anything people have said about you. I realize I was tactless at times myself... I should have been more careful..." He was almost stammering. "Are you planning to take the post that was advertised in Copenhagen?"

"Please don't blame yourself, Soren! I'm not leaving because of anything that anybody said. I would have told you sooner, but I felt you might not understand. You see, I'm not going to Copenhagen—I'm going to Jerusalem."

"Jerusalem! Whatever will you do there?"

"I don't know—but I believe that's where God wants me."

"Lydia, I never thought you would carry these new ideas of yours to such extremes!" Soren was half angry, half bewildered. "Do you really think...?"

"No, Soren, I don't think—and I don't know—but I *believe!* For years I built my life on my own planning and reasoning, but I've found there's another dimension to living!"

"Another dimension, Lydia?" Soren's voice sounded strangely flat. "That's something I don't understand."

The class bell rang. I reached out my hand and caught his for a moment. "I have to go now, Soren! I'm sorry!"

As I reached the turn of the corridor, I glanced back. Soren was still standing where we had parted, following me with his gaze. The next moment I had rounded the corner and he was out of sight. I had gone less than fifty yards from him, and yet I knew that I had walked out of his life.

Inside me there was a pain too deep for tears. I thought that death itself could not have made the separation more final. My mind went back to my baptism. I had recognized it even then as a burial, but I had not seen its full implications. My relationship with Soren had brought so much happiness to us both. Was it also part of the old life that I must lose before I could find the new life into which God was leading me?

I still had to tell Mother of my resignation, but I knew a letter would not be sufficient. I waited until the weekend of Pentecost and made a quick trip to Brønderslev. On Saturday morning I told Mother as simply as I could what I had done. When I had finished, she sat silent for several minutes.

"But," she said at last, "what will you *do* in Jerusalem?"

"Mother, I've asked myself that question many times. And yet I believe God has a special work for every person—and somehow I will find mine in Jerusalem."

I returned to Korsør with a deeper respect than ever for my mother. My news had shocked her deeply, yet she had avoided saying anything that might have made it more difficult for me to follow the course I believed to be right. I began to pray that God would prepare her for the time that I would actually leave for Jerusalem.

Term ended in mid-July. At first it was hard to realize that I was no longer a teacher. One practical reminder was the fact that I received no more salary checks. Life seemed strangely empty. However, I could not afford to dwell on the past. I began to make such plans as I could for my journey to Jerusalem. In a missionary magazine published in Sweden I had noticed the address of a Swedish lady who lived in Jerusalem. Her name was Ida Gustafsson. I decided to write and tell her I was coming to Jerusalem.

While waiting for her reply, I started to sell my furniture. The prices I was offered were ridiculously low, but I had no desire to bargain. Half the money that came in I gave to the Pentecostal people for furnishings they needed for their church. I also gave them my piano. The rest of the money I set aside for my journey to Jerusalem and for my expenses on arrival there.

The only items of furniture that I held back were my bed, a chair, and an occasional table, which I wanted to give to Valborg. I knew that she would have no trouble in finding work, but I gave her an extra month's salary. "Thank you, Miss, for everything," she said. "I'll think of you every night I sleep on your bed—and I'll say a prayer for you, too!"

One day, as I was sitting alone in the almost-empty apartment, Kristine Sonderby came to the door. In addition to her familiar black purse she carried a flat, paper-wrapped package. "I haven't come to buy anything," she explained, "I just wanted to bring you this..."

Pulling the paper from her package, she held out an unframed picture with a tear-off calendar fitted in a slot at the bottom. The picture, in pastel colors, showed a shepherd in biblical attire, with a staff in one hand, holding a newborn lamb in his other arm. Under it, in Gothic lettering, were the words, "He shall gather the lambs with his arm, and carry them in his bosom" (Isaiah 40:11). Kristine peered at me uncertainly through her thick lenses. "I still don't understand everything you've told me, but I'll be praying for you."

After Kristine left, I laid the calendar on top of a pile of things I had put out ready to pack for my journey. It was a type of sentimental church art that I particularly disliked. "But at least," I said to myself, "there'll be two people in Korsør praying for me—Kristine and Valborg."

The first Sunday in August, at the morning service in the Pentecostal church, I met a big-boned woman with a mass of straw-colored hair loosely held in place by two tortoiseshell combs. She was Kitty Sorensen, a missionary from China. She told me that she was planning to start her journey back to China at the beginning of September. We agreed that we would travel together as far as Egypt—by train across Europe to Marseilles, and then by boat to the port of Alexandria on the north coast of Egypt. From there Kitty would continue on the ship through the Suez Canal to the Orient, and I would complete my journey by train across the Sinai Peninsula to Jerusalem.

Ten days later I received a reply from Miss Gustafsson, the Swedish lady in Jerusalem. She was delighted to learn of my plans, she wrote, and offered to meet me on arrival, if I would let her know by what route I was coming. Her reply encouraged me greatly. At least I would have a home to go to on arrival in Jerusalem. I wrote back outlining my plans for the journey and promising to send a telegram from Alexandria.

On Friday, September 21, I went to the travel agent and paid for my ticket to Alexandria. Out of the money I had left I kept a bare minimum for my expenses in Denmark until the end of the month and converted all the rest into $180 worth of traveler's checks. That was the sum total of my worldly wealth.

The next Monday I sent my main luggage ahead to Copenhagen, while I myself caught a train to Brønderslev. I had promised to spend my last few days in Denmark with Mother.

For our first two days together, Mother and I simply enjoyed each other's company. By an unspoken agreement we made no reference to the events that had followed my baptism or to the unknown future that awaited me in Jerusalem. Eventually, on the afternoon of my last day at home, Mother herself broke this self-imposed silence.

"Since you were here last, I've been thinking about something that happened when you were a little girl of five," she said, rocking gently to and fro in her favorite chair. "You were so very ill with pneumonia, I thought we were going to lose you. I remember standing by your bed one night and telling God that if He would spare your life, you would be His. Perhaps that explains some of the things that have happened these last two years."

"Yes, Mother, it helps me to understand, too." I gave her a kiss on her forehead, then slipped out to make some last-minute preparations for my journey to Copenhagen the next day.

By the time I came back, Mother had dozed off with her head resting against the back of the rocking chair. I stood several minutes in silence, enjoying the familiar beauty of her features. She had aged noticeably in the last year. Much of that, I knew, was due to her concern about me.

Suddenly she opened her eyes and looked up at me. "Isn't that strange!" she exclaimed. "I must have dozed off—and then I saw your face in front of me. You looked just like you did as a little girl of five—with those long gold ringlets you used to have. I wonder why I should see a thing like that!"

"I think God is showing you something, Mother," I said. "He's showing you that I haven't really changed. I'm the same little girl you've always known.

Only now I'm beginning to find the real purpose that God had for me all along."

At the supper table later that evening Mother spoke briefly of her concern for my future. "But at any rate, I'm happy for one thing," she added.

"What's that, Mother?"

"I know you're not without money. You should be able to live for more than a year on the money you inherited from Father."

"There's no need for you to concern yourself about that, Mother, or about anything else," I replied hastily. "There are only two things I want you to do—to write regularly and to pray for me every day." How grateful I was that Mother had not asked me how much I had left from Father's legacy. It would have been hard to tell her that I had given the last of it away to a hospital in the Congo!

The next morning Mother and Anna both accompanied me to the station. When the time came for me to board the train, Mother held me in her arms for several moments without speaking. Finally she said, "You're still my little girl, the sweetest in the world!"

As the train began to move out, Mother ran alongside until she could no longer keep up. Then she drew out her white lace handkerchief and stood waving it. I kept my eyes fastened on her until she finally merged into the background. The last thing I was able to see was the white handkerchief, still waving.

6

THE JOURNEY

The next morning I met Kitty at the main station in Copenhagen. Through a melee of passengers hurrying to and fro, and porters pushing barrows laden with great cabin trunks, we made our way to the train that was to take us to Marseilles. About a dozen friends of Kitty's had gathered to see her off, and she leaned out the window carrying on an animated conversation—punctuated at intervals by the hiss of steam escaping from the engine. I stood behind her in the carriage, trying to appear cheerful, but inwardly I was acutely aware that there was no one there to see me off.

"And why should there be?" I reminded myself. "Kitty is a missionary under appointment, returning to her field. But you're not a real missionary, you're just..." I paused, unable to complete the sentence, even in my own mind. No church or missionary society was sending me, so I couldn't be a missionary. What was I, after all?

The final whistles blew and the train moved out. Kitty and I settled down into two corner seats opposite each other. "Now we're really on our way!" Kitty remarked, pushing her tortoiseshell combs back into place. Again I found myself comparing my position with hers. She was making a journey that she had already made once before, returning to an established mission in a country that she knew well. But for me the journey was the first step into a totally new and unknown world.

I tried to fight off a numbing sense of fear, hoping that Kitty was not aware of my inner struggle. Involuntarily, I clutched my purse more tightly: In it were my passport, my ticket on the ship to Alexandria, and my $180 in traveler's checks. After all, I reflected, I would have Kitty's company as far as Alexandria, and Ida Gustafsson's home to go to in Jerusalem.

When night came on, we each retired to a third-class sleeping bunk. For a while the remorseless clatter of the train wheels pounding their way southward kept me awake, but eventually I dozed off. Suddenly I found myself standing in front of a large desk. Opposite me a dark-complexioned man was seated, with his elbows on the desk and his chin cupped in his hands. His black eyes were fastened on me, as though awaiting the answer to a question. Under the pressure of his continuing stare I averted my eyes to a strange object that stood on one corner of the desk. It was made of stiff, red cloth, in the form of a truncated cone, and a black silk tassel, attached to its top, hung down one side. Conscious of the man's eyes still fastened upon me, I searched for an answer to his question, but my throat was dry and no words came to my lips.

Suddenly the train gave a lurch, and I was aware of the bunk curtains swaying in front of my eyes. I realized that I had been dreaming. Yet this realization did not dispel the emotional impact of the dream. I could not banish from my mind the dark features and the black eyes of the man behind the desk, nor that strange red hat with the black silk tassel. The sense of embarrassment and helplessness did not leave me. It was another hour before I succeeded in getting to sleep again.

The next morning I related my dream to Kitty, but she could make no more of it than I—except to say that the red object sounded like the tarboosh worn by government officials in Egypt.

It was a relief when the train finally drew into Marseilles. Neither Kitty nor I knew more than a few words of French, but we succeeded in taking a taxi to a small hotel not far from the harbor. We were shown to a little bare room with two single beds.

"None too clean," Kitty commented, "but it'll do for a couple of nights until we get on board our ship for Alexandria."

The next morning we went to the office of Thomas Cook to make arrangements for boarding the ship, which was due to sail the following afternoon. In my halting English I told the clerk that I planned to disembark in Alexandria, and he asked to see my passport. "If you are getting off in Egypt," he said, "you will need a visa from the Egyptian government. You won't be allowed off the ship without one."

"Where can I get a visa?" I asked.

The clerk gave me the address of the Egyptian Consulate.

Leaving Kitty to finish her business at Cook's, I took a taxi there alone. After a brief wait, I was ushered into the consul's office.

"Good morning, madam," he said in English. "What can I do for you?"

"Good morning—" I began, but the words froze on my lips. Seated at the desk in front of me was the very man whom I had seen in my dream on the train two nights before. There was no mistaking the swarthy features and the black eyes fastened on me, exactly as I had seen them in the dream. Automatically I glanced at the far corner of the desk, but even before I did so, I knew with an inner certainty what would meet my eyes. Sure enough! There was the strange red headgear with the black silk tassel! Every detail was exactly as I had seen it in my dreams.

With an effort I turned my eyes back to meet those of the consul, aware that he was still awaiting an answer to his question. Eventually I forced the words through my lips. "I've come for a visa. I'm on my way to Palestine, and I need a visa to get off the ship at Alexandria." I dug down in my purse, then pulled out my passport and handed it to the consul.

He flipped the pages of the passport casually, then said, "We can't issue visas here. I shall have to write to Cairo."

"But—but won't that take a long while?"

"About two weeks. Maybe longer."

"Two weeks!" I exclaimed. "But I can't wait two weeks; my ship sails tomorrow." The emotional impact of my dream came back upon me with its force redoubled. My throat was dry and my tongue like lead. "Can't you please do something to help me?"

"Madam, there is nothing I can do." The black, unyielding eyes were still fastened upon me.

"But you don't understand!" I said. "If I don't catch that ship, I'll be left here in Marseilles—on my own. I know no one here. I'm just..." I felt the tears rising to my eyes, and my voice trailed off into silence.

"I repeat, madam, there is nothing I can do." The consul held out my passport. Like a person hypnotized, I took it from his hand and left the office.

On the sidewalk I stood for several minutes trying to take in the situation. Finally—because I could think of nothing else to do—I took a taxi back to Thomas Cook's. There was no sign of Kitty. She must have concluded her business and returned to the hotel.

I told the clerk what had happened at the Egyptian Consulate.

"Without a visa you cannot sail on the ship to Alexandria," he said. "The only thing I can suggest is that you take a ship that sails from Marseilles to Tel Aviv."

At the mention of Tel Aviv my heart leaped. From studying the map in Korsør, I recalled that it was a port on the coast of Palestine, even closer to Jerusalem than Alexandria was. "Is there any ship going soon?" I asked.

The clerk looked for a few minutes in his files. "There's a French ship leaving in one week," he said. "Its destination is Tel Aviv. But it will be calling at various ports along the way. We could obtain a passage for you on that ship."

"How much would it cost from here to Tel Aviv?"

Again the clerk looked in his files: "Forty-six dollars."

"Could I exchange my ticket on the ship to Alexandria for one on the ship to Tel Aviv?"

"I'm sorry, madam," the clerk replied, "but we have no authority to exchange or refund your ticket to Alexandria."

Apparently I had no alternative. I would have to buy a ticket on the French ship to Tel Aviv. I drew the folder of traveler's checks out of my purse and carefully counted out $70. I paid $46 for the ticket and with the other $24 I purchased French money. If I could keep my expenses below $4 a day, this would cover the extra week I would be obliged to spend in Marseilles. But my folder of traveler's checks felt pitifully thin as I slipped it back into my purse. More than one third of my money had already gone!

Back in the hotel I told Kitty what had happened. When I had finished, she sat silent for a while, her fingers busy with her tortoiseshell comb. Eventually she broke her silence: "It isn't easy to understand why God should permit a thing like that, but at least you can hold on to one thing, Lydia—God showed you in advance through your dream what was going to happen."

"Then you really believe that my dream came from God?"

"Indeed I do. If God can show you beforehand every detail of a situation that lies ahead, then you know that He is still in control of the situation, no matter how your own plans may be upset."

I hung eagerly on Kitty's explanation. It was like the proverbial silver lining to the dark cloud of disappointment that had overshadowed me. My mind began to adjust to the new situation. I went over to a rickety table by the window and wrote a letter to Ida Gustafsson, the Swedish lady who had promised to meet me on my arrival in Palestine, explaining the unexpected change in my plans. I gave her the name of the French ship on which I had now booked my passage, together with its expected time of arrival in Tel Aviv. Would she come so far to meet me? There would be no time to receive an answer from her in Marseilles.

Kitty went with me to the post office. The clerk there, who spoke English, informed us that an airmail service had recently been inaugurated to Palestine. That would give my letter a good chance of reaching Miss Gustafsson in time. From the post office we took a walk around the area near the harbor, pausing to gaze into shop windows and trying to translate French francs into Danish kroner.

After lunch the next day I accompanied Kitty to her ship and helped her carry her hand luggage down to the cabin. There were only two bunks, and the one above Kitty's was empty. No doubt it was the one in which I should have been traveling. When Kitty had put her things in place, we knelt down side by side at Kitty's bunk and committed each other to God's care and protection.

At 4:00 PM a bell sounded, warning all visitors to go ashore. Up on deck Kitty gave me a final embrace, then watched me descend the gangplank. From the dockside I could still see her standing on deck. She had her hand cupped to her mouth, apparently trying to tell me something, but she was too far away for me to hear her.

Eventually, with several blasts of its sirens and clouds of black smoke billowing from its funnels, the ship began to move away. As long as I could see Kitty on the deck, I continued waving to her, but in a few minutes a change in the ship's course hid her from sight. I still followed the ship with my eyes as it made its way out of the harbor and onto the open sea. Gradually it dwindled to a black silhouette against the background of a sky that was luminous with the last rays of daylight.

Suddenly I was gripped with an overwhelming sense of loneliness. My separation from Kitty had severed my last contact with Denmark. I was in a strange city where I knew no one and could not understand the language. I had nothing to look forward to but six days by myself in a very bare hotel bedroom. Up to that moment, I had never really known what it was to be alone. Now loneliness settled down upon me like the damp air of dusk. I began to shiver slightly.

My thoughts turned to Denmark. I wondered what Mother would be doing at that moment. I pictured her moving gently to and fro in her rocking chair, keeping time with the rhythmic click of her knitting needles in her hands. It seemed so natural to hear her voice: "My little girl, don't you see it's dark? Go back quickly to your hotel!"

With a shock I realized that it *was* dark. Back home in the northern climate of Denmark I had never seen night fall so swiftly. But now I was alone in the darkness, a solitary woman in a strange city. I started walking as fast as I could back to Marseilles.

Halfway to the hotel I heard heavy footsteps behind me. Then a thick voice said something in French, and I felt a man's hand on my hip. Instinctively I turned and said, in Danish, "Leave me alone!"

I was face-to-face with a burly man in a sailor's uniform. For a moment that seemed like an age, I smelled the alcohol on his breath and I listened to my own heart pounding as if it would burst. Then he shrugged his shoulders and his arm dropped to his side.

I felt a strong urge to start running, but I did not dare to show how afraid I was. I walked on about fifty yards and then glanced back over my shoulder. The man was still looking in my direction, but he made no attempt to follow me. Five minutes later, flushed and out of breath, I was back in my hotel bedroom.

I cast myself down beside my bed and tried to pray, but no words came. Instead, deep sobs forced themselves out of my throat. At last the sobbing subsided and was followed by a profound inner silence. Time itself seemed to stand still. The past and the future were both excluded. I was poised in an eternal "now."

After an unmeasured period of this inner stillness the words of an unknown language began to flow spontaneously from my lips. With a shock I realized that I was not speaking them, but singing them—with a melody like that of some medieval church chant. Although I could not understand the words, I had no doubt of their theme. It was one of worship and rejoicing, even of triumph. I rose from my knees and began to walk to and fro with my hands uplifted and the words of the chant still flowing from my lips.

By this time it was quite natural for me to speak in an unknown language. In fact, I did it nearly every time I prayed. But this was the first occasion on which the Holy Spirit had given me not merely words I did not understand, but also a melody I had never heard. Surely this was further proof—if proof were still needed—that all this did not come from my own mind. Indeed, with my mind I still did not understand why I should be worshipping God with such a triumphal chant in that bare little room. Outwardly nothing had changed, and yet inwardly fear and loneliness had given place to peace and joy.

I picked up my Bible from the nightstand, intending to read once more my favorite verse in Romans that began with the words, "Likewise the Spirit also helpeth our infirmities..." (v. 26). However, my eyes focused instead two verses down from it: "And we know that all things work together for good to them that love God, to them who are the called according to his purpose" (Romans 8:28).

Called according to his purpose... Those words applied to me! It was God who had called me to leave Denmark and take this journey. I was seeking to find and fulfill His purpose for my life. But if so, then all that had happened was for my good! The disappointment, the delay, the extra expense, the loneliness—all of it had been permitted by my heavenly Father for my own good!

Here was indeed reason to worship and to rejoice—reason that my mind could accept. But, in God's order, my spirit had begun to rejoice before my mind had understood the reason for it.

For the rest of my stay in Marseilles, my hotel room became my prayer closet. No longer did it seem bare or lonely. It took on an atmosphere that was almost sacred. Each day I spent hours there, alternately worshipping and praying—sometimes speaking, sometimes singing—sometimes in an unknown language, sometimes in my own.

In that atmosphere of prayer I began to understand the various ways in which God had protected and cared for me. Through my dream on the train He had shown me that He knew what lay ahead, down to the minutest detail, even though I did not. Then, at the moment of loneliness at the dockside, He had spoken to me in the accents of Mother's voice. Could anything have shown more clearly the tenderness of His love for me? Finally, He had shielded me from the man who accosted me in the street.

Beyond all that, however, I came to see why God had permitted the change in my plans. For years I had been so self-reliant, so strong in my own wisdom and judgment. In my career as a teacher this had served me well enough, but in my new walk of faith it had become a hindrance. Now I was stripped of my self-reliance and cast upon the mercy and faithfulness of God. No longer would I depend on my own judgment to plan each step that I was to take. I was content to place my hand in God's and let Him lead me, day by day and step by step.

The French ship sailed punctually at noon on Monday, October 8, 1928. I remained on deck watching the outlines of Marseilles drop down over the horizon. It was exciting to be once again on my way to Jerusalem. Yet I knew that the lessons learned in Marseilles had been worth the time that I spent there.

I quickly discovered that no one on the ship understood Danish. This meant that I was obliged to start using English as my daily language. Most of the crew members were French and most of the other passengers were Arabs from various parts of the Middle East, but nearly all had some knowledge of English. If at times they found my English phrases strange, or my heavy Danish accent hard to understand, they were too polite to show it.

I became friendly with a merchant from Amman, who introduced me to the Arabic language. He was the first Arab with whom I tried to share my faith.

"How do you say the name of Jesus in Arabic?" I asked him.

"*Ya-su-a,*" he replied.

"And what's the word for this?" I asked, touching a door.

"*Bab,*" my friend replied.

I already knew that the Arabic word for "God" was *Allah.*

"*Ya-su-a bab Allah,*" I told him, pointing up to heaven as I spoke. "Jesus is the door to God."

He smiled politely and nodded his head.

Our journey eastward was a leisurely one. We called at various ports on the north coast of the Mediterranean, and also at one of the Aegean islands, many of the place-names bringing to mind Paul's missionary journeys.

During the voyage I spent some time studying a secondhand map of the Holy Land that I had picked up in Denmark. I noted that the main road from

Tel Aviv wound eastward through the mountains to Jerusalem. According to the scale on the map, the distance would be about fifty miles. The main mountains seemed to cluster near Jerusalem. I was reminded of the words of the psalmist: "As the mountains are round about Jerusalem, so the LORD is round about his people from henceforth even for ever" (Psalm 125:2).

Our ship berthed at Tel Aviv on the afternoon of Thursday, October 18. Standing at the ship's rail, I had my first close view of the Holy Land. The dock beneath me was littered with crates and bales, between which sailors and porters ran to and fro, gesticulating and shouting at one another in a language I took to be Arabic. Opposite, there stood a long, sprawling shed, with a sign that read H.M. CUSTOMS & IMMIGRATION. Below were words in two different kinds of lettering, both unfamiliar to me. Arabic, perhaps, and Hebrew?

By standing on tiptoe I could just glimpse, over the roof of the shed, a motley group of people clustered on an open patch of sandy ground. Presumably they were waiting to meet passengers from the ship. Could one of them be Miss Gustafsson? There was no way to tell.

One of the sailors helped me get my luggage off the ship and into the customs shed. My first interview was with an officer of the Immigration Department. "You're from Denmark?" he said. "A visitor?" I nodded.

He flipped through the pages of my passport, then pressed his rubber stamp down on an empty space. "I've given you a visitor's visa—valid for six months," he explained. At the bottom of the imprint, in small letters, I noticed the words NOT A WORK PERMIT.

Next a customs officer asked me to open my two main items of luggage—a suitcase with my clothes and a wicker trunk with bedding and a few items of silverware and kitchen equipment. After rummaging for a few minutes in the trunk, the officer marked both pieces of luggage with blue chalk and allowed me to pass on.

A moment later I found myself outside, with my luggage at my feet. The first sight that met my eyes was a man in a tattered tunic, lying on the sand against the wall of the shed. The skin of his feet and legs was eaten away by open sores. Noticing that I was looking at him, he stretched out toward me an arm that ended in a raw, red stump, repeating in a monotonous whine a single word, "Bakhsheesh—Bakhsheesh—Bakhsheesh."

I could not take my eyes from the sores and the raw stump. Could that be *leprosy?* Right there in the open, without any dressing, and with the flies swarming over it! I opened my purse to find a coin, then realized that the only money I had was French.

Before I could decide what to do next, I was surrounded by a cluster of ragged urchins, all screaming and gesticulating at the same time. One thrust a picture postcard in my face; another held out a tray of trinkets and souvenirs; a third knelt at my feet as if to shine my shoes. Out of the corner of my eye I saw a tall, elderly lady, with iron gray hair, striding toward us. "She could be a Swede," I thought to myself.

"Are you Miss Christensen from Denmark?" the lady said in Swedish, pushing the urchins aside with practiced skill.

"Yes," I answered in Danish, "I'm Lydia Christensen. You must be Miss Gustafsson. It's most kind of you to come and meet me."

"Welcome to the Holy Land!" Miss Gustafsson said, clasping my outstretched hand with her bony fingers. "Did you have a good journey?" Without giving me an opportunity to answer, she continued, "If we're to get to Jerusalem today, we've no time to lose. Wait here with your things while I find a taxi."

As I stood waiting for Miss Gustafsson to return, I surveyed the scene before me—the leper, the ragged urchins, the swarms of flies, the sand littered here and there with empty cans and rotting fruit. Over it all there hovered a vague, unfamiliar smell that made my stomach turn slightly. I could imagine no title for such a scene less appropriate than the "Holy Land."

Before long Miss Gustafsson returned with a taxi. There followed a lengthy conversation in Arabic between her and the driver. I understood that they were bargaining about the price for the trip to Jerusalem. Both of them sounded as if they were angry. I wondered if they would come to blows, but in the end they obviously reached an agreement. "Could that be the normal way to conduct a conversation in Arabic?" I asked myself.

The driver bundled my luggage into the trunk, and we set out on the journey to Jerusalem. As we were leaving the outskirts of Tel Aviv, night came on. Once again darkness caught me by surprise, as it had done on the dock in Marseilles. One moment, it seemed, the sun was shining, and a few minutes later everything was dark.

I noticed, too, that as soon as darkness came on, the streets were emptied of people. Even when we passed through a town with houses on either side, there was no one to be seen out in the streets. Once we left Tel Aviv, there was no kind of public lighting, even in the towns.

As my eyes adjusted to the dark, I could see that all the windows were protected by wooden shutters. Every now and then the dim rays of a lamp filtered out through a crack in the shutters, but this feeble light served to accentuate, rather than to dispel, the surrounding darkness. I could not help contrasting it all with the brightness and security of even a small Danish town at night, and a strong sense of homesickness swept over me.

"Why are there no people out in the streets?" I asked.

"Oh, people never go out after dark!" Miss Gustafsson exclaimed. "They would be attacked and robbed, perhaps even killed!" She gave a nervous high-pitched laugh.

"Aren't there any police to protect people?" I asked.

"Oh, yes, there is a police force, modeled on the British pattern—quite efficient in its colonial way. But if you were attacked in the street at night, they would probably take the attitude that you had only yourself to blame for being out at such an unreasonable hour! A legacy from Turkish times." Again her words were followed with that rather tense laugh!

The road began to wind upward, and I was conscious of the dark outlines of mountain ridges on either side. "We must be starting the climb to Jerusalem," I thought. My pulse began to beat a little faster.

After a while we came to a place where the road seemed to be doubling back on itself all the time. "These bends are known as the Seven Sisters," Miss Gustafsson explained. "We're not too far from Jerusalem now."

I was aware of a dark mass of mountain on one side and what seemed to be a sheer drop into nothingness on the opposite side. The driver took each bend with the barest margin between us and the edge of the road. Each time we made a turn, the car rattled and swayed and the tires emitted a smell of burning rubber. From time to time Miss Gustafsson would lean forward and speak to the driver. "*Shwoya–shwoya!*" she said. "*Shwoya–shwoya!*"

Then she turned and explained to me, "That's the first word you need to learn for when you travel by taxi in this country. It means 'slowly' or 'carefully.'"

I repeated the phrase over to myself several times to have it ready for future use.

My day had been tiring, and I began to doze. I was awakened by Miss Gustafsson saying, "This is the outskirts of Jerusalem." At once I was wide awake. "We're on the Jaffa Road," Miss Gustafsson added. "It will take us right into the center of the city."

The air was calm and the sky cloudless. By this time the thin crescent of a new moon was visible, adding a little to the light that filtered down from a myriad of stars, and I could make out the outlines of the houses with surprising clarity.

"How quiet everything is!" I commented. "And how solid the houses look!"

"They are solid," Miss Gustafsson replied. "They're all built of hewn stone. No other material is permitted within the city."

She leaned forward and said something in Arabic to the driver. "I've asked him to go a little out of our way," she explained. "The route we are going to follow will take us to the northwest corner of the Old City and down the west wall—past the Jaffa Gate. That will make a good introduction to Jerusalem for you."

A little further on, the road broadened out before us. "Allenby Square," Miss Gustafsson explained. "That dark mass of stone right in front of us is the wall of the Old City."

I strained my eyes to pick out the rows of hewn stone rising up to a jagged line that cut across the night sky. The taxi veered slightly to the right, and we continued for about a quarter of a mile with the dark shadow of the wall on our left. "What a strange combination of silence and strength," I thought. "It almost makes a person feel like an intruder."

Miss Gustafsson touched my arm and pointed to the left. "That tower there rising above the wall is the Tower of David," she said. "That's where the Jaffa Gate stands. But of course it's been closed and barred since the sun went down."

Shortly after passing the Jaffa Gate the taxi turned right over a bridge and up two or three steep inclines. "This is Talbieh—the district where I live," Miss Gustafsson said. Again she spoke to the driver in Arabic.

Eventually we came to a stop in front of a narrow rectangular build-ing. The driver set my luggage down on the sidewalk, and Miss Gustafsson counted some money into his palm. No ray of light from outside or inside illu-minated the building, but Miss Gustafsson obviously needed no light. Picking up my suitcase, she led the way to a heavy iron door level with the sidewalk. I followed behind her, holding my wicker trunk with both hands in front of me.

Miss Gustafsson pulled a large iron key from her purse and opened the door. After groping around in the hallway, she found some matches and lit a kerosene lamp. Holding the lamp in her left hand, she led the way into the living room. The stone floor was partly covered by a threadbare rug. The fur-niture was Victorian in style, dark and dusty. The air was close and permeated by some indefinable smell that reminded me of a secondhand clothing store.

"My bedroom is in there," Miss Gustafsson said, pointing through a half-open door at one end. "I'll make up a bed for you here on the sofa."

She fetched two narrow sheets from a closet and stretched them over the sofa. Then she covered them with a faded patchwork quilt. For a pillow she stuck a straw cushion under the sheet at one end of the sofa. I had had nothing to eat or drink since lunch, and I was desperately thirsty.

"Could I have a glass of water?" I asked.

Miss Gustafsson looked at me as though my request was unreasonable in the extreme. "Water?" she said. "Why, certainly not! The water is contami-nated. If you drink it, you will be sick."

Well, probably I was tired enough to sleep in spite of my thirst. "Perhaps we could open a window," I suggested. "The air is so closed in here."

Once again Miss Gustafsson fixed her dark eyes upon me with a stare that added double emphasis to her words. "Open a window?" she said. "Never! The snakes would come in!"

An involuntary shiver went down my spine. "Are there really snakes as close as that?"

"Indeed there are! And that's not all!"

At the end of each remark there came that strange, high-pitched laugh. It was beginning to affect my nerves. "Contaminated water! Snakes lurking outside the window!" I said to myself. "What else could there be?" But I was too dismayed to ask any further questions.

As soon as I stretched out on the sofa, Miss Gustafsson went to her bedroom, taking the lamp with her. A few minutes later I heard her blow out the lamp.

I lay in the dark, desperately trying to ignore my thirst, but it only grew worse. I remembered that on a table in the corner of the room I had noticed a pomegranate in a dish. If only I could open it and suck a mouthful or two of the juice, I felt that I could hold out until the morning.

Stealthily I rose from the sofa and tiptoed toward the table. As I stretched out my hand for the pomegranate, the sleeve of my nightdress brushed against an earthen pot on the near side of the table. It fell to the stone floor with a resounding crash and broke into fragments. A bloodcurdling scream came from the bedroom, and the next moment I saw the form of Miss Gustafsson in a long white nightdress outlined against the blackness of the bedroom door.

"Thieves!" she screamed. "Thieves! They've broken in! Thieves!"

"No, Miss Gustafsson," I tried to reassure her, "no one has broken in. I was trying to get something off the table, and I knocked down the pot. I'm sorry!"

"Oh, it's you!" she said. "Thank God for that! I'd forgotten you were here."

She turned back into her bedroom, and I continued groping until I located the pomegranate. I had no knife with which to cut it open, but I dug my nails into its flesh and succeeded in splitting it open with my fingers and sucking out a small quantity of rather acid juice.

I tiptoed back to the sofa and lay down. Tired though I was, I could not relax. I was occupied with Miss Gustafsson. Were her fears real? Or were they fantasies of a mind affected by many years of living alone in Jerusalem? How long would my own nerves hold out?

Meanwhile, it was clear that Miss Gustafsson really did not have accommodations for more than one person. Her narrow, straw-stuffed sofa was no substitute for a proper bed.

Unconsciously I began to pray. "Lord, if You have another place—a place that You have chosen for me—please lead me to it *quickly*!"

But where could I even begin to look? Apart from Miss Gustafsson, I did not know the name or address of a single person in the whole city. A cloud of dark emotions settled down over me—loneliness, homesickness, insecurity—all compounded by the musty atmosphere of Miss Gustafsson's living room.

Eventually I fell into a restless sleep. But in my dreams I saw myself in a taxi driving wildly around hairpin bends, pursued by a screaming figure in white who cried, "Thieves! Thieves! Thieves!"

7

JERUSALEM

In the morning I noticed that Miss Gustafsson was careful to boil every drop of water we drank, but the coffee she served for breakfast at last brought relief to my thirst. I was determined to move away from her living room as soon as possible, but I had no idea where to go. I recalled my prayer of the previous night. Did I really believe that God would quickly show me where I was to live?

"Miss Gustafsson," I said as we finished breakfast, "I need to pay you back for the taxi and your other expenses yesterday. Could you tell me where I can cash some traveler's checks?"

"The best place is Barclays Bank," she replied. "It's in Allenby Square. We passed it last night. I have some business there myself."

The sun was shining strongly out of a cloudless sky as we set out for the bank. From the outset I determined to learn all that I could about the city to which God had brought me—even though I still did not know what He had for me to do there.

"How dry and dusty everything looks!" I commented.

"We've had no rain since April," Miss Gustafsson replied, "but we're due for a heavy rainfall within the next month—what the Bible calls 'the first rain.'"

Fifty yards ahead of us a small flock of sheep and goats was grazing in a vacant lot beside the road. A young man in a long white tunic stood watching them, leaning on the top of a staff. He was protected from the sun by a red-and-white scarf, fastened with a black cord around his head.

There was something strangely familiar about the young man. Yet I knew I had never seen him before. Suddenly I caught my breath and stopped dead on the sidewalk. My mind went back to the men I had seen in my vision, sitting on the rock. The scarf on the young man's head was checkered, not pure white, and the cord around it was black, not gold. But otherwise his style of dress was identical. It was hard to contain my excitement. This really must have been the land that God showed me in my vision!

"That's the traditional Arab costume," Miss Gustafsson commented, noticing my interest. "Most Arab men still wear it, but some are beginning to wear suits of a Western style."

We came to a wide road with a sign at one corner that read KING GEORGE V AVENUE. "That's the main street running north and south through the New City," Miss Gustafsson said. In this area I noticed that most of the people were dressed in European style. Within the space of a hundred yards I heard snatches of conversation in several European languages, as well as one or two that sounded Asian.

"Jewish immigrants," Miss Gustafsson explained. "Since the war they've been streaming in—which the Arabs resent bitterly. Tension is building all the time. Before long there's going to be an explosion."

Ten minutes later we reached Allenby Square. In the bright sunlight the Old City wall was less aloof and mysterious, and the area below it was now filled with noise and activity. But behind it all the impression of silent, changeless strength was as powerful as ever.

As we entered the bank, I began to debate with myself how many of my traveler's checks I should cash. I hated to see them dwindle too quickly. Eventually I cashed forty dollars, for which I obtained approximately ten Palestinian pounds. I gave Miss Gustafsson four pounds (just over fifteen dollars) for the taxi and the other expenses of her journey to Tel Aviv and thanked her most warmly for all that she had done for me. This left me with six pounds (just under twenty-five dollars) in cash, and sixty dollars in traveler's checks. How long would that last me?

When I had finished my business, Miss Gustafsson took her turn with the cashier. She had some problem about a draft from Sweden that had gone astray. While waiting for her, I walked out onto the steps of the bank to watch the people in the street. Perhaps one of them was the woman with the jar on her head...

Almost immediately I picked out a woman on the opposite side of the square standing in the shadow of the wall, one hand supporting the jar on her head. Could she really be the one? I scanned every detail of her clothing and her features. Certainly she was dressed the same way, but there was no scarf around her hips. Besides, the woman on the rock was lighter complexioned and considerably younger. Excitement mingled with disappointment. No doubt I was in the land—but I had not seen the very woman.

"Sorry to keep you waiting!" Miss Gustafsson said as she joined me on the steps a few minutes later. "We'll go back home another way. I have to visit a missionary over there in Abu Tor." She pointed vaguely southward. "Her name is Lorna Ratcliffe. The two of us are responsible for the refreshments at the monthly inter-mission fellowship."

With her long strides, Miss Gustafsson set out straight across Allenby Square toward the point where the Jaffa Road bent southward along the west wall of the Old City. I almost had to run to keep up with her.

Before long we found ourselves part of a stream of men and animals that occupied the full width of the road. Donkeys and camels, monstrously laden with sacks or wicker baskets, jostled ruthlessly against us. The men leading them belabored them unmercifully with sticks and hurled at them savage words that sounded like curses. Every now and then a man would stagger past carrying on his bent back a burden that I would have considered too heavy for a donkey.

"On their way to the markets inside the Old City," Miss Gustafsson said.

At that moment a bale on a passing donkey struck me so forcefully in the back that it nearly knocked me off my feet. "The principle of 'Ladies First' doesn't seem to apply in this part of the world," I said.

"Indeed not!" Miss Gustafsson snorted. "It's just the other way around. You see that man with the cane in his hand—and the woman behind him with the big bundle on her head? That's the order in this land! The man goes in front at his ease and the woman follows behind, carrying everything!"

"Why does she have that black veil over her face?" I asked.

"Because she's a Muslim," Miss Gustafsson answered. "It's considered indecent for a Muslim woman to show her face in public."

On one side of the road a man stood with a large brass vessel like a pitcher strapped to his back. From the top of the pitcher a long, fine spout protruded over one shoulder. In one hand he carried a metal cup, and in the other hand two small brass plates. He continually clapped the brass plates together with his fingers, making a loud metallic sound that advertised his presence. At the same time he kept crying, *"Moya barideh! Moya barideh!"*

"Cold water," explained Miss Gustafsson. "He's selling drinking water."

At that moment a customer came up to the man with the pitcher, who quickly bent the upper part of his body forward and deftly caught in the metal cup a fine stream of water that was propelled out of the spout of the pitcher by the motion of his body. Then he handed the cup to his customer to drink, and received in exchange some small metal coins. I waited to see if he would wipe the cup before the next customer came up, but he did not. Altogether the idea of actually selling water was new to me. It added greater meaning to Christ's promise to give "the water of life freely" to everyone who was thirsty. (See Revelation 22:17.)

When we reached the Jaffa Gate, most of the people turned to enter the Old City. We paused for a moment to watch them surging through the gateway like the waters of a broad river suddenly confined within a narrow gorge. Then we continued southward, passing a shallow pool of brown water on our right. Miss Gustafsson turned back for a moment here and pointed toward the southern wall of the Old City. "That's the Hill of Zion," she said, "but of course Zion is often used as a name for the whole city. The word goes back to the days of David."

About a quarter of a mile further on we turned to the left and followed a dusty road that wound up a steep incline to a cluster of houses at the top. "This is where Miss Ratcliffe lives," Miss Gustafsson said, stopping outside a two-story house with a flat roof. She led the way up a short flight of steps and knocked loudly on the iron door. The door was opened by a dark-skinned woman in a long, full dress that fell in loose folds over her bare feet. She exchanged greetings in Arabic with Miss Gustafsson and led us through a wide entrance hall into a room furnished partly as an office and partly as a living room.

A short, gray-haired lady rose up from behind a wooden rolltop desk and came to greet us. She appeared to be in her late fifties. She was wearing a long-sleeved dress in a dark gray material that completely covered her body from her neck to her ankles. The only relief from the gray was provided by a narrow, starched white collar and white cuffs.

Miss Gustafsson began the introductions. "Miss Ratcliffe, this is Miss Christensen. She's just arrived from Denmark."

"From Denmark? What brings you all the way to Jerusalem?" Miss Ratcliffe's voice was soft, but surprisingly deep. "Are you a missionary?"

"Well, not exactly. But I believe God has brought me to Jerusalem for some purpose..." I paused, wondering if Miss Ratcliffe thought me as foolish as I sounded to myself.

"Are you staying in a hotel—or with friends?"

"Miss Gustafsson was kind enough to let me spend last night on her sofa, but I don't really have a place yet."

Miss Ratcliffe's eyes seemed to size me up. "I have a room in my basement that's empty. Would you like to have a look at it?"

Like a person in a dream I found myself following Miss Ratcliffe down an inside staircase to the basement. She opened a door and led the way into a large room with walls and floor of stone. I paused in the doorway and cast my eyes quickly around. It required only a moment to take in the details. The walls and the floor were completely bare, but two wooden doors in one corner gave an indication of some kind of closet behind them. The entire furniture consisted of four articles—a bed and a chest of drawers on the left, and a table and a chair on the right. At the far end there was an iron door, and to the left of the door a heavily barred window, through which I glimpsed the outline of a stone staircase.

As my eyes took in these details, a warm glow filled me. It was the same sensation that I had first experienced in Korsør when I began to pray about going to Jerusalem. Was the Holy Spirit telling me, "Now you're hot!"?

The inner warmth was in strange contrast with the bare scene that confronted me. Could this really be the place that God had prepared for me? I recalled my prayer of the previous night. I had asked God to show me where I was to go—*quickly*. If this was God's answer, it had come far more quickly than I had expected.

Miss Ratcliffe's voice broke in upon my thoughts. "That iron door opens onto a sunken courtyard, and there is a staircase from there up to the street. So you would have a private entrance of your own, without having to go through our part of the house."

"Miss Ratcliffe," I answered, "everything has happened so suddenly that I really don't know what to say."

"Why don't you take a little while to pray about it before you decide?" And in another moment she was gone.

Left to myself, I knelt down beside the bed to ask God for a clear answer. Unconsciously, I began to picture my living room in Korsør—the green velour chair, the Wilton carpet, the walnut piano, the gold brocade curtains. The pressure of the stone floor against my knees seemed to reinforce the contrast with my present situation. What could God have for me to do in such a place?

I could find no answer to this question, and yet I still felt that strange, comforting warmth within me. I remembered the decision I had made in the hotel in Marseilles. I would no longer rely upon my own reasoning to plan my way. I would simply put my hand in God's and let Him lead me step by step.

"Father," I said, "if You have led me to this place, then I am content to be here." The moment I uttered these words, my inner questioning ceased. I knew that I was in the place of God's appointing. I rose to my feet and returned to the living room to accept Miss Ratcliffe's offer.

"Splendid, Miss Christensen," she answered. "When would you like to move in?"

Before I had time to answer, Miss Gustafsson broke in. "She can move over today. We'll go straight back to my house and get her things. She doesn't have much, anyhow."

By four o'clock that afternoon I was installed in Miss Ratcliffe's basement. My few dresses were hanging on one side of the closet in the wall. Some shelves on the other side accommodated my items of kitchen equipment. The rest of my clothing and accessories fit easily into the rickety chest of drawers. A yellow chenille bedspread added a welcome touch of color to the black iron bedstead. In front of the window, my wicker trunk, emptied of its contents, did duty as an extra piece of furniture.

Some previous occupant had left a rusty iron nail in the wall above the bed. That seemed the right place to hang Kristine Sonderby's calendar with the picture of the shepherd.

Just as dusk was coming on, Miss Ratcliffe came to my door with a lighted kerosene lamp. "Here is something you will be needing," she said. "When you have time to buy one of your own, you can return this to me." She placed the lamp on the table and sat down on the chair. "Tell me more about how you came to Jerusalem," she continued.

I seated myself on the wicker trunk and began to tell her how Christ had revealed Himself to me in Denmark and how I had eventually given up my position as a teacher and set out for Jerusalem. "Even now," I concluded, "I still don't know what God has for me to do here."

"Ten years ago I, too, came to Jerusalem without knowing what I would find waiting for me," Miss Ratcliffe replied. She went on to describe the work that had been gradually built up—a Sunday school, a women's Bible class, evangelism in the prisons and among British soldiers and policemen.

She paused to adjust the lamp, and her face was momentarily illumined by its rays. A network of tiny wrinkles gave evidence of many years' exposure to the sun.

"They have been ten difficult years," she said, "with many heartaches and disappointments. But then our Lord Himself warned us what to expect, when He said, 'O Jerusalem, Jerusalem, which killest the prophets, and stonest them that are sent unto thee' [Luke 13:34]. Indeed there is no other city in the world like Jerusalem."

"Are you sorry, then, that you came?"

"No, Miss Christensen, I'm not sorry. In spite of everything, Jerusalem is her own reward. She demands that you love her so completely that no suffering or discouragement or danger can ever change your love for her." She smiled. "That's why the psalmist said, you know, 'If I prefer not Jerusalem above my chief joy.'"

When Miss Ratcliffe eventually got up to go, I held her back. "There's one thing you haven't told me yet," I said. "What will be the rent of my room?"

Miss Ratcliffe looked at me with the suspicion of a smile. "Shall we say eight dollars a month?"

When she had gone, I placed my Bible on the table beneath the lamp and turned to the book of Psalms. I wanted to read for myself the words that Miss Ratcliffe had quoted concerning Jerusalem. Eventually I found them:

If I forget thee, O Jerusalem, let my right hand forget her cunning. If I
do not remember thee, let my tongue cleave to the roof of my mouth;
if I prefer not Jerusalem above my chief joy.   (Psalm 137:5–6)

I closed the pages of the Bible and looked around me. The bare severity of
the walls was softened a little by the shadows. A deep sense of peace seemed
to settle down over the room. This was my new home! How grateful I was to
be here! I bowed my head in worship.

"Thank You, Lord!" I said. "Thank You that I am here in Jerusalem!"

———————

The next morning Miss Ratcliffe invited me up to have breakfast with her.
As we were eating, she began to offer me some advice about settling in.

"One of the first things you should do is rent your own postbox," she said.
"Mail delivery to street addresses is unreliable. Then of course you're going to
need some groceries—and a Primus."

"A Primus," I said, "what's that?"

"A small stove that uses kerosene. It's what most people in Jerusalem cook
with."

Miss Ratcliffe picked up a little brass bell that stood beside her plate and
tinkled it two or three times. A door opened behind her, and a woman came in
and stood by her chair. I recognized the same dark-skinned woman who had
answered the door the previous day.

"This is Maria," Miss Ratcliffe said. "She doesn't understand much
English, but I'll tell her where to take you and what you need to buy." She
turned and spoke to Maria in Arabic.

"I've asked her to take you to the post office first," Miss Ratcliffe explained.
"Then you can walk down to the Damascus Gate and come back through the
Old City. You'll be able to pick up the things that you need in the markets
there. Maria will handle the money for you."

Five minutes later Maria and I were walking side by side toward the
center of Jerusalem. On top of her head Maria had a small, tightly wound coil
of cloth, upon which rested a shallow, circular basket woven out of reeds. I
was reminded once more of the woman with the jar on her head in my vision.

Apparently it was normal for Arab women to carry things on their heads in this way, without any conscious effort on their part.

Maria knew only a few words of English, but she was able to point out the main places of interest. We retraced the route that I had taken the previous day with Miss Gustafsson, following the Jaffa Road northward. At Allenby Square a right turn brought us to the post office, where, for the sum of four dollars, I rented a box of my own for the next twelve months. Continuing eastward along the north wall of the Old City, we came to a broad, arched gateway with a wide, cobbled expanse in front of it.

"Damascus Gate," Maria said.

In the area in front of the gate several groups of animals were clustered—sheep, donkeys, and camels. For some distance on either side, the walls were lined with wooden stalls on which stood rows of sacks with open mouths. In one section the sacks contained various types of coarsely ground flour. A little farther on I saw sacks with rice, sugar, and lentils. Other stalls were piled high with firewood or charcoal.

Leaning against one of the stone pillars of the gate was a man with a large wicker basket strapped to his back. Maria beckoned to him, and he fell in behind us as we passed through the gate. Soon we were in a maze of narrow cobbled streets that cut their way between rows of small stores. In some places the streets were covered over with stone arches; in others the walls of the houses on either side jutted out so far as almost to meet over the center of the street. Beneath, a kind of artificial twilight prevailed. I wondered how anyone could find his way through it all, but Maria seemed quite at home.

Each section had its own characteristic form of merchandise. There was one street for tinsmiths and other metal workers, another for shoemakers. I noticed one area where rugs and carpets were displayed, and another set aside for china, glass, and pottery. We passed through a long section with fruit and vegetables, and then one where various kinds of freshly butchered meat were displayed. Swarms of flies hovered around the meat, but no one seemed concerned to drive them away.

As I was standing in front of a butcher's store, waiting for Maria, a man pushed past me with a barrow and tipped out onto the stone floor a pile of sheep's heads—freshly decapitated and skinned. Before I had time to adjust to this spectacle, a second man followed with a larger barrow containing the sheep carcasses. I wondered whether I would ever again be able to eat mutton and enjoy it!

At one corner Maria pointed down a street where there was hardly any activity visible. "*Yahoud!*" she said. "Jews!" She pillowed her head on her hands in the position of one resting. I realized that it was Saturday, and the Jews were celebrating their Sabbath.

In all the other areas, however, the noise and activity were intense. Men and animals pressed their way ceaselessly in both directions through the narrow channels of the streets. Inside the stores, customers bargained noisily with merchants, watching them narrowly as they weighed their goods on metal scales suspended from the ceiling.

In addition to the harsh sounds of an unfamiliar language, the air was filled with a strange medley of pungent odors—hyssop, pepper, roasting coffee, frying fat, freshly baked bread, the garlic on everyone's breath, the sweat of men and beasts, and the droppings of innumerable animals. The total impact upon my senses was more than I could take in.

I noticed that there were no prices marked on any of the items. Each purchase that Maria made required a period of animated discussion before she handed over any money. If she was not satisfied with the prices in one store, she moved on to the next. The idea of bargaining over the price of a pound of potatoes or a dozen eggs was absolutely new to me. Obviously, time was of little importance here. The man with the basket followed us patiently from stall to stall. After each purchase was complete, he bent his body forward with the mouth of the basket toward Maria, and she placed her purchase inside.

Eventually the three of us emerged into a more open area leading to a high iron gateway, which Maria identified as the Jaffa Gate. By this time the basket on the man's back was full. At the bottom, its outline just visible through the wickerwork, was a four-gallon can of kerosene. Piled on top of this was a miscellaneous assortment of groceries—tomatoes, cucumbers, potatoes, black olives, goat cheese, a paper sack of sugar, as well as some vegetables I had never seen before. At the top of the pile was the Primus stove, a dustpan, a large box of matches, and three glass bottles—containing milk, olive oil, and methylated spirits. Protruding above all the rest was the head of a broom, its handle wedged down between the groceries.

In addition, Maria carried in the basket on her head some flat, round loaves of brown bread and a dozen small eggs. In one hand she carried a lamp with a bowl and a chimney of glass. My share of the total burden was tiny, but very important to me—the key of my newly rented postbox, which I had tucked securely into my purse. In the midst of so much that was new and strange, that little key somehow linked me still to Denmark.

Passing through the Jaffa Gate we emerged into the full sunlight once again. It took me a few moments to adjust my eyes to the glare from the dust and the rocks. A few yards down the road, I turned back and allowed my gaze to follow the wall of the Old City northward. I had not realized how many different colors there were in the wall. The stones of the Jaffa Gate itself ranged through various shades of gray, but those in the wall to the north of it had a delicate tinge of brown that glowed warmly in the sunlight.

When we got back to Miss Ratcliffe's house, the man with the basket followed us down the stone stairs to the courtyard, where he knelt down patiently while Maria lifted her purchases out of his basket. By now I was not surprised at the noisy discussion between him and Maria that followed. Obviously they were settling his wages for the morning's work. Finally they seemed to reach an agreement, and the man took his leave, tucking the money away somewhere inside the folds of his loose garment. I got the impression that he was well satisfied with the amount he had received, but that he did not wish to show it.

I thanked Maria warmly for her help and then settled down to the task of putting away all that we had bought. The smaller items went on the shelves; the large ones I arranged as neatly as I could on the floor beside the closet. Finally I took my new broom and swept the floor.

———————

Miss Ratcliffe had explained to me briefly that Palestinian currency was based on the decimal system. A *pound* was divided up into a hundred *piastres*, and a piastre in turn was divided into ten *milliemes*. When I had my room in order once more, I made an account of what I had spent, as follows:

Groceries	89	piastres (about $3.56)
Kerosene	28	piastres
Methylated spirits	6	piastres
Lamp	47	piastres
Primus	62	piastres

| Broom and dustpan | 17 | piastres |
| Man with basket | 15 | piastres |

| | 264 | piastres (about $10.76) |

This left me with about fourteen dollars in Palestinian money and sixty in uncashed traveler's checks. I began to calculate how much longer this would last me, but then decided that it was a waste of time. My resources were obviously going to be exhausted before long. A week or two one way or the other would not make too much difference.

In the afternoon Miss Ratcliffe came down to see how I was getting on. I took the opportunity to question her about the water supply, mentioning what Miss Gustafsson had said about contamination.

"Well, the situation isn't quite as bad as that," Miss Ratcliffe replied with a smile. "Down through the centuries Jerusalem has always had a problem with water. Today, city water is pumped to some areas. But almost all houses built in the Turkish period have underground cisterns in which they catch rainwater from the roof. That's what we have here. Over the years, I suppose, my stomach has gotten used to it—at any rate, I don't normally boil my water."

Later that day Maria gave me my first lesson in using a Primus. First she filled the tank with kerosene. Then she poured methylated spirits into the trough at the top, and ignited it. Finally, with quick movements of the pressure pump, she forced the kerosene up a vertical pipe and out through the perforations in the head, where the heat from the methylated spirits produced a clear blue flame that burned with a steady hissing sound.

That evening I did my first cooking on the Primus—two boiled eggs. To these I added a salad of lettuce, tomato, and cucumber, a loaf of coarse bread, some goat cheese, some olives, and a cup of hot tea. I softened my bread by dipping it in olive oil, but I could not persuade myself that oil would ever take the place of good Danish butter!

With my meal ended, I cleared the table and, in the circle of light cast by my new lamp, I spread out my Bible and the map of Jerusalem. First, I carefully traced on the map the route that Maria and I had followed that day—up the west side of the Old City, along the north wall, down through the Damascus

Gate, then westward to the Jaffa Gate, and back along the west end of the Valley of Hinnom.

After that, I opened to the book of Psalms and began looking for verses that referred to Jerusalem. After a while I was arrested by these words: "Thou shalt arise, and have mercy upon Zion....For thy servants take pleasure in her stones, and favour the dust thereof" (Psalm 102:13–14).

Stones and dust. How real these words now were! But—could a person actually fall in love with things like that?

I paused again: "Our feet shall stand within thy gates, O Jerusalem" (Psalm 122:2). That morning my feet had done that very thing!

"Pray for the peace of Jerusalem," the psalmist continued, "they shall prosper that love thee" (Psalm 122:6). How much God's people in those days had to say about love for Jerusalem! Their relationship to the city was so personal—almost like that of a child to his mother, or a young man to his bride.

Later, when I knelt in prayer before retiring to bed, my mind returned to this theme. "Thank You, Lord, that You have brought me to Jerusalem," I said again. "I do not understand why I am here, and I do not feel worthy to be here. But please help me to love this city as Your servants have loved her down through the centuries."

Lydia and her eight daughters
First row, left to right: Johanne, Magdalene, Elisabeth, Anna, and Kirsten. Second row, left to right: Peninah, Tikva, and Ruhammae

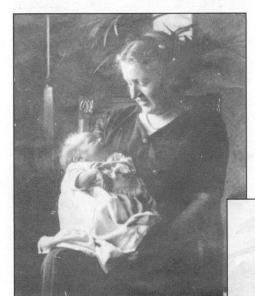

Lydia in her twenties in Denmark, holding her niece

Lydia with one of her sisters

Lydia with Johanne

Jameela, Lydia's Arab helper, with
one of the children from the home

Lydia with girls from the
children's home

On the balcony of her home in Jerusalem

With Arab children in Ramallah

Lydia with Jesika, their ninth daughter

Lydia with Elisabeth and Anna

With soldiers and children
from the home

Derek as a young soldier in the
English army

Lydia and Derek in Ramallah

On a visit to Denmark

Lydia and Derek
in London

Lydia and Derek in the early 1970s

With their London congregation

Derek and Lydia ministering in San Antonio, Texas

With John Hagee (playing the saxophone)

Lydia, Derek, and their eight girls

Lydia's daughters at her funeral
Left to right: Magdalene, Elisabeth, Tikva, Johanne, Jesika, Ruhamma,
Peninah, Anna, and Kirsten

Lydia Christensen Prince (1890–1975)

8

MY PLACE

The next day was Sunday. I attended Miss Ratcliffe's morning service, which was held in a long, narrow room on the first floor. There were about twenty-five persons present, mostly women and children. A group of children sang some lively choruses in Arabic. One of these I identified as the Arabic version of "Jesus loves me! this I know." Then a British policeman in uniform gave a talk on the importance of reading the Bible each day. He was interpreted by an Arab who apparently was also a policeman.

That afternoon I wrote a long letter to Mother describing my journey and my first impressions of Jerusalem. I decided that from then on I would write to her without fail at least once each week. I also wrote letters to Valborg, Kristine Sonderby, and Pastor Rasmussen, giving them my new address.

In the days that followed, I began to develop a pattern of living that was suited to my new surroundings. Recognizing my need to be more systematic in my daily Bible reading, I divided the Bible up into three main sections: the historical books, from Genesis through Esther; the poetical and prophetical books, comprising the remainder of the Old Testament; and the New Testament. Each morning I began my day by reading from the New Testament; in the middle of the day I read from the historical books; and at night I closed the day with a reading from the poetical or prophetical books.

In addition, I picked out certain themes that related to my new situation: the city of Jerusalem, the power of prayer, the various forms of service for God—since I was seeking to discover my own appointed service in Jerusalem and up to then it was mainly through my prayers that God had directed me. I chose a pencil of a different color for each theme—blue for Jerusalem, green for prayer, red for service—underlining each passage in the appropriate color. At the end of the day I compared the passages underlined in the same color from the three main sections of the Bible, and I was continually impressed by the way in which they cast light upon each other.

Another need I recognized was to improve my knowledge of English. I decided I could combine this with my Bible reading. I put my two Bibles side by side, reading first in the Danish and then in the English.

As soon as I felt I had mastered a new phrase, I would try it out in conversation with Miss Ratcliffe. From time to time I brought a smile to her lips by saying that I had "girded on" my coat or "kindled" my Primus—and she laughed aloud when I told her that "my bowels had moved with joy!"

In addition, I set aside time to pray for my former colleagues at the school in Korsør. Recollecting how they gathered each day in the common room for their midmorning coffee break, and making allowance for the difference in the time zone, I made it a point to pray for them at that very time, asking God that He would somehow make Himself as real to them as He had to me.

It was not long before Miss Ratcliffe approached me about the need of language study. "The sooner you start learning the language of the country," she said, "the better."

"What language would you advise me to start with?" I asked.

"It's no use learning Hebrew—hardly anyone speaks it," Miss Ratcliffe replied. "The Jews born here speak mainly Arabic. The ones who have immigrated speak the language of the country which they came from—and some form of Yiddish. Arabic is the language you will need most. The lady who played the piano on Sunday morning is a language teacher."

I arranged with the Arab lady to give me five one-hour lessons a week for the sum of two dollars. After my first two weeks I was ready to give up. Some of the sounds, especially the gutturals, were unlike anything in my own language or any other language I had ever heard. My throat ached with the effort of trying to pronounce them. The script was equally unfamiliar, running from right to left, with three different forms for each letter—according to whether it occurred at the beginning, the middle, or the end of each word. The vocabulary was no less formidable. My teacher mentioned that there were actually forty different Arabic words to describe a camel. The rest of my life, I felt, would not suffice to master a language like that!

In the midst of my struggles with Arabic, help and encouragement came to me from an unexpected source. In addition to Maria, there was an older, blind Arab woman, named Nijmeh, who also lived with Miss Ratcliffe. Through association with various missionaries, Nijmeh had acquired a good knowledge of English. She regularly read an English Braille Bible and delighted to quote from it by memory in her dry, husky voice. Like many blind people, she compensated for her lack of sight by a heightened sensitivity in other areas.

With nothing to help her but her little white cane, Nijmeh would make her way down to the Old City and spend an hour or two there each day. She had a knack of getting into conversation with people, and nearly always ended by sharing with them her faith in Christ. "I call these my fishing trips," she explained. "I try to obey the words of our Lord—to be a fisher of men."

Nijmeh had both the time and the patience that was needed to help me in my struggles with Arabic. Each day after my teacher left, Nijmeh made me review with her the new words and phrases over and over again until my pronunciation satisfied her. Frequently I repeated a word twenty or thirty times before Nijmeh exclaimed, *El-hamd il-Allah!*—"Thanks be to God!"—indicating that I had reached the required standard.

I often accompanied Nijmeh on her "fishing trips" as far as the Jaffa Gate and then went on by myself to explore the area outside the walls of the Old City, stopping at the post office to see if there was a letter from Denmark. But the box was always empty. More than once I saw a woman who reminded me of the one in my vision, but never the very same woman. I came to the conclusion that it was not wise to be too much occupied with her. If God intended me to meet her, He would arrange it in His own way and time.

On my way back from one of these trips, I ran into a Jewish funeral procession. Four men walked ahead, carrying a stretcher on which the body was laid out, wrapped in a tasseled prayer shawl. The mourners straggled behind. The men came first, clothed in black, their heads covered by black, broad-brimmed hats. Behind them the women, with their disordered hair flowing loosely over their faces, let out a continuous high-pitched wailing cry. In the eyes of men and women alike there was a set stare of blank and hopeless grief. Never had I seen people demonstrate such a horror of death... How desperately they needed to know the One who said outside the tomb of Lazarus, "I am the resurrection, and the life" (John 11:25)!

At last—after I had been more than three weeks in Jerusalem—I found a letter from Mother in my postbox. My hands trembled as I opened it. I read it through without even pausing to relock the box. Mother's letter was full of local news. Inge, the postmaster's daughter, had married an American sailor. Hans Peter, my childhood playmate, had been appointed manager of our local savings bank. When I came to the closing phrase, my eyes blurred with tears. Mother had signed herself, "Your loving—and praying—Mother."

On my way back from the post office that day I stopped at a bookstore and bought myself an Arabic Bible. I now had three Bibles to set out on my table side by side: the Danish, the English, and the Arabic. One day I proudly told Nijmeh that I had read my first Bible verse in Arabic.

"Which verse was it?" she asked.

"The first verse of the gospel of Saint John."

"How long did it take you?"

"About two hours."

"El-hamd il-Allah!" was Nijmeh's comment.

One morning in mid-November, just a month after my arrival in Jerusalem, I awoke with a strange impression that the world around me had changed. The air was filled with a steady, drumming sound. At first I did not understand exactly what the change was. Then it suddenly dawned on me—it was raining! I could see it through the iron bars of my window.

For several minutes I stood at the window fascinated, unable to take my eyes from the rain. It did not come down in drops, but in a solid sheet, filling my whole field of vision. This was the first time I had seen rain since I set foot in Palestine. It was the long-awaited "first rain," breaking a drought that had lasted since April.

The rain continued without a break the whole of that day and on into the night. The temperature in my room dropped more than twenty degrees. The wall and the floor exuded a fine film of moisture. When I drew my finger across them, it left a path in the dampness. At night it took all the blankets I had brought with me from Denmark to keep me warm, and for my early-morning Bible reading the next day I found it necessary to wear my overcoat.

In my walks through the Old City I recalled passing a street where various kinds of oil-heating stoves were displayed. When the rain eventually ceased, I made my way to this street, walking in thick, shoe-clogging mire where two days previously there had been only dust. I did my best to follow Maria's pattern of shopping, walking around various stalls and asking the prices in each. Eventually I found a stove that looked suitable and offered the man half the amount that he had asked. To my surprise he accepted immediately! I realized he had been expecting me to start much lower.

I picked up my stove by the handle and started back home. Passing a man with a basket on his back, I was tempted to let him carry my stove for me. But I made a quick mental calculation. I had paid $4.32 for the stove. This left me with about $3.00 in my purse and $30.00 in traveler's checks. I decided I had better carry the stove myself!

At the end of November I received a letter from Valborg:

> Last Sunday I went to the Pentecostal church and Pastor Rasmussen prayed for me and I spoke in tongues! Now I understand what made you so happy—even when everybody was against you....
>
> You will never guess where I am working now—with Miss Storm. She came to me a month ago and asked if I would work for her. She keeps asking me questions about you and what made such a change in your life. To tell the truth, I think she's interested, but doesn't want to show it....

"That means that from now on I must pray twice as much for Erna Storm!" I commented to myself.

From time to time, as I watched my supply of money dwindle, I considered the possibility of finding a job of some kind. Perhaps there was a school somewhere at which I could do at least some part-time teaching. But I was reminded that my visitor's visa was not a work permit. Should I try to get my visa changed? Each time I thought of doing this, I lost my inner peace. The Holy Spirit, I understood, was telling me, "Now you're getting cold." If only God would give me some indication of the work that He had for me to do!

Two weeks after Valborg's letter I received one in an unknown handwriting, postmarked from Beirut in Lebanon. Who could be writing to me from Beirut? I knew no one there. The letter was in Danish. Under the heading DANISH MISSION TO BIBLE LANDS, it read,

> Dear Miss Christensen,
>
> Your name has been given me by Mr. Pedersen, principal of the government school in Korsør. He tells me that you served under him

as director of the domestic-science department, but that you are now in Jerusalem.

I am writing to ask if you would accept a position in charge of domestic science at our girls' school here in Beirut. We have about two hundred pupils enrolled, and we wish to expand our domestic-science department. Under suitable direction we feel that this could become a most important part of our ministry to the people of Lebanon.

Lebanon is an attractive land, with an excellent climate and scenery unrivaled in any part of the world. Your salary would be on a scale set by the Mission Board. It would be less than you received as a government teacher in Denmark, but all your personal needs would be met, and after ten years' service you would qualify for a pension scheme.

Please give this proposal your careful consideration, and let me hear from you as soon as possible.

Yours sincerely,
Martha Ditloffsen, Principal

Each time I read the phrase *domestic science*, my heart beat a little faster. After all, that was the field in which my interest had lain so long. What a challenge to introduce the subject to girls in a less-privileged land! I began to think of ways to adapt and simplify the methods that had been so successful in Korsør. Could it be that God was really opening a door for me in Lebanon? I had been two months in Jerusalem, and nothing had opened up here. My money was almost exhausted and no one seemed to need me.

I read the whole letter through twice. Then I tucked it into the back of my Danish Bible. In the days that followed I took it out and read it through again several times, but I could not decide how to answer it.

After the first heavy fall of rain that marked the beginning of winter, the weather followed a more variable pattern. There were days that were bright and sunny, interspersed with squalls of wind and rain. At times the rain would fall steadily for eight or ten hours without a break. One day a brief flurry of snow reminded me that Christmas was only a week away.

I had received Christmas cards from my two sisters in Denmark, some of the teachers in Korsør, and a few other acquaintances. There was not a word from Soren. I received only one gift—a beautiful light blue sweater that Mother had knitted for me herself.

This would be the first time in my life that I had spent Christmas away from home. Normally I looked forward to Christmas with a sense of excitement and anticipation that had not changed since childhood. But this year the approach of Christmas filled me with a sense of dismay—almost of foreboding. Miss Ratcliffe had invited me to share dinner with her on Christmas Day, but for me the real time of celebration had always been Christmas Eve. How could I celebrate that alone in a cold, stony basement, without a friend or a relative to share it with me?

I sat down and took stock of my financial position. I had cashed my last traveler's checks a few days previously. Out of the proceeds I had paid Miss Ratcliffe the rent of eight dollars due her for December. I was also up-to-date with my payments to my Arabic teacher. After laying in a supply of groceries and of fuel for my lamp and my stove, I had about four dollars left. For some reason that I could not explain to myself, I felt that I must make my money last through Christmas. After that—well, who knew what might happen?

About 4:30 PM on Christmas Eve, I lit my lamp and set about preparing my Christmas dinner: a small piece of mutton cooked in olive oil over my Primus with potatoes and eggplant—though I still had to struggle against the memory of those sheep's heads on the butcher's floor! My dessert was a kind of sweet, sticky pastry called *bakalawi*, which I had recently discovered in the Old City. I rounded off the meal with a cup of strong coffee. (I had learned the art of brewing coffee over a Primus in the Danish way.)

As I sipped my coffee, I began to picture my family gathered at home. I could see the long dining table, laden from end to end with all the delicacies I had loved since childhood. My sister Ingrid's husband was walking from chair to chair, pouring the dark red wine into the crystal glasses, while at the far end Kezia's husband, Knud, was lifting the paper flags from the goose's breast. I tried to visualize Mother—but somehow I could not. I longed for a glimpse of her face.

There came the same overwhelming sense of loneliness that I had first experienced standing on the dockside in Marseilles. I struggled against the tears that rose to my eyes. With an effort of will I cleared away the remains of my meal and placed my Danish Bible on the table. This evening I had no heart for English, much less for Arabic. I wanted only my mother tongue.

As I opened my Bible, the letter from Beirut dropped out. I did not need to read it. I could repeat its phrases by memory: "...a position in charge of domestic science....Lebanon is an attractive land....All your personal needs would be met...." Was this really the job that God had waiting for me all along—with Jerusalem just a stepping stone to Beirut?

My Bible reading the previous evening had concluded with Psalm 136. I turned to the next psalm and began to read. It was the one I had read on my very first evening in this basement room:

> If I forget thee, O Jerusalem, let my right hand forget her cunning. If I
> do not remember thee, let my tongue cleave to the roof of my mouth;
> if I prefer not Jerusalem above my chief joy.   (Psalm 137:5–6)

Did I really mean that? If so, the question was settled. I had asked God to show me the place He had appointed for me—and He had done so. It was Jerusalem—not Beirut, nor any other place in the world. Nothing could change that! If it meant loneliness or even starvation, then I would starve where God had placed me. But my commitment was to Jerusalem. No personal desire or ambition must ever take precedence over that!

There was one way to settle the issue. I got out my pad and started a letter to Martha Ditloffsen in Beirut. At first I struggled for words, but gradually they came. I thanked her for her letter and her attractive offer but explained that my calling from God was to Jerusalem—and to Jerusalem alone. In conclusion, I wrote, "I must confess that I do not know yet what work God has for me to do in Jerusalem, but I can only seek to trust Him and obey Him as He leads me step by step."

After addressing and sealing the envelope, I laid it on my chest of drawers, ready to take on my next trip to the post office. Then I turned and looked at my room. Nothing had changed, and yet it looked so different. The plain wooden furniture, the stone floor, the barred window—no matter how bare or how simple, it was my place! I was here in obedience to God. Nothing else mattered! I began to feel the bubbling of inner joy that I knew came from the Holy Spirit.

My eyes fell on the broom standing in one corner. I remembered how I had danced with one the night God had filled me with the Holy Spirit in Korsør. The floor did not need sweeping, but I had to give expression to the feeling that was bubbling up inside me. I picked up the broom and began making vigorous sweeping movements toward the door.

"Out you go, *doubt!*" I said, pushing my broom across the floor. "There's no place for you here! And you, too, *loneliness.*" (Another thrust with the broom.) "And *depression*—and *compromise!*" (Several more swipes with the broom.) "Out you go, all of you! I'll have no more of you!"

I paused for a moment and leaned on the broom to catch my breath. Suddenly another thought came to me. "And that goes for you, too, *self-pity!*" I said, with a final sweep.

Then I looked around the room once more. "After all," I said to myself, "the first Christmas was celebrated in a stable. What you have here tonight is luxury by comparison!"

My eyes were drawn toward the Bible, still open under the lamp. Walking over to the table, I picked up my blue pencil and carefully underlined the verses I had just been reading. When I came to the last phrase, I drew a double line under it: "if I prefer not Jerusalem above my chief joy."

9

THE FIRST TASK

It was the Friday after Christmas—a gray, bleak day. I had just finished my midday meal when I heard the sound of footsteps descending the stone staircase in the courtyard. I looked out through the window in time to glimpse a pair of trouser-clad legs. The next moment there was knock at the door.

Opening the door, I found myself face-to-face with a bearded man of medium height, apparently in his early thirties. He was dressed in a shabby, European-style suit, and on the back of his head he wore the traditional Jewish yarmulke, or skullcap.

"Good afternoon," he said. "Are you Miss Christensen?"

Too surprised to speak, I nodded. How did he know my name?

"My name is Cohen," he continued, "Eliezer Cohen. My wife and I have a baby daughter who is dying. I have come to ask if you will take her." His English was slow and heavy.

"A dying baby?" I said. "But—but I know nothing about babies. How did you even know I was here?"

"My wife and I—we believe in God. We prayed: 'God, show us what to do!'" The man placed his hands in a position of prayer and looked upward. "This morning my wife met a blind woman at the Jaffa Gate, and she said that a very kind lady from Denmark had come to Jerusalem and was living in the basement of this house. Aren't you the lady?"

Nijmeh! But whatever made her give my name to these people? Aloud I answered the man, "It's true I came from Denmark, but I'm not a nurse or anything like that."

"What did you come to do? Didn't you come to help us?" There was the urgency of desperation in the man's voice. It was the very question I had asked myself a hundred times: *What did I come to do?* But surely God was not asking me to take a dying baby—in that bare basement.

"I really don't mean to be unhelpful," I said, "but I'm not in a position to do anything for you. I have no place to put your baby—no medicine for her, no food, and no money to buy any! You should take the child to the hospital."

"We've already done that," the man replied, "but the hospital won't take her. They say there is nothing they can do for her. She was one of twins. The other twin died two months ago, and now this one is dying, too! It's affecting my wife's mind. She can't stand it any longer!"

"Mr. Cohen," I said, "it isn't that I don't want to help. I just don't see what I can do." At that moment I caught the look in his eyes, the same blank, hopeless stare that I had seen in the eyes of the people in the funeral procession. "At least—you must give me time to pray about it. Then, if I find I can do anything, I will come and see you. Where do you live?"

He gave me directions for finding the house, and I promised to get in touch with him if I could see any way to help him.

Reluctantly, the man began to take his leave. Halfway up the stone stairs, he turned and said, "Please don't wait too long!"

A few minutes later my Arabic teacher came to give me a lesson, but I found it impossible to concentrate. At the end of the lesson I paid her the two dollars I owed her for the week. When she had gone, I emptied the change from my purse onto the table and counted it: eighty-six cents. That was all I had!

Soon afterward Nijmeh came down to review my Arabic lesson. "Nijmeh, did you meet a Jewish lady at the Jaffa Gate and tell her that I would take her sick baby?"

"Well, I did meet a lady there this morning who sounded like a Jewess. She was in great distress about her baby, and I told her about you."

"But, Nijmeh, what made you think that I could help her?"

"Miss Christensen, I have been praying for years that God would send someone to care for the children in this city who have no home. I believe you are that person."

I stared at her in amazement. "Me, Nijmeh? But surely there are some children's homes in Jerusalem."

"Yes. Orphanages—big institutions. But I don't know of any place that I would call a *home*, where a child would really feel loved and accepted."

"But, Nijmeh, I have no place to put even one child—no money, no mission behind me..."

Nijmeh rose and began to feel her way toward the door. "I will continue to pray." A moment later I heard the tapping of her cane as she made her way up the stairs.

"But this is insane," I said to myself. "Even the hospital won't take this baby. What can I do?"

As I turned this over in my mind I recalled a passage that I had underlined in my reading from the New Testament that morning. I opened my Bible and turned to the last chapter of the epistle of James. Five verses, from 14 through 18, were underlined in green—the color that I used for *prayer*. One sentence in particular seemed to leap from the page: "And the prayer of faith shall save the sick" (v. 15). Was God telling me that prayer could still save the life of the child—even when all human resources had been exhausted?

Almost afraid of the answer I would receive, I bowed my head over the table and said, "Lord, please show me if it is Your will for me to take that baby."

Several minutes of silence followed. I could hear my watch ticking away the seconds. Then there came to my mind a single sentence from Christ's parable of the sheep and the goats: "Inasmuch as ye have done it unto one of the least of these my brethren, ye have done it unto me" (Matthew 25:40). The words were so clear and direct that it was almost as if the Lord Himself had spoken them to me audibly.

I looked down at my watch—almost 4:00 PM. Less than an hour of daylight remained. Too late to try to find Mr. Cohen's house that evening. I would go first thing the next morning. But now another voice came to me—the voice of Mr. Cohen as he turned and looked back from the stairs in the courtyard: "Please don't wait too long!"

I walked to the window, trying to decide what to do. The precious minutes of daylight were passing. Out of my conflicting thoughts there was one I could not turn aside: *If the baby should die tonight, I would have to answer for her to God.*

"Lord, help me not to fail You," I whispered. Then I grabbed my overcoat from the closet and started up the stone stairs, buttoning my coat as I went.

Half walking, half running, I made my way up the Jaffa Road as far as Allenby Square. From there on I had to go more slowly, looking for the landmarks that Mr. Cohen had given me for direction. About a quarter of a mile further on I passed a large building on my right, flying the Union Jack. That must be the law courts. Now there should be a street off to the right. Yes, there it was! Mr. Cohen's house was the third one on the left.

Climbing a few cracked stone stairs, I knocked on the door. In the silence that followed I could hear my own heart pounding. Then the key turned in the lock, and the door opened a few inches.

"Who is it? What do you want?" asked a man's voice.

"It's me—Miss Christensen," I said. "You asked me to come."

The door opened wide. Mr. Cohen stood in the opening, his yarmulke still on his head. "At last!" he said. "I thought you were never coming!"

Without further words he led the way into a large, dimly lit room. The floor was paved with crude, ill-fitting stones. The ceiling was arched in a style that dated from Turkish times, rising from four corners to a low dome in the center. The damp, cold air, combined with the shadowy domed ceiling and the uneven floor, created the impression of a cavern rather than a room.

A frail-looking woman sat hunched on an iron bed, her head and shoulders wrapped in a coarse black shawl. "This is my wife, Hadassa," Mr. Cohen said. "She doesn't speak English."

Mr. Cohen led the way to a small iron crib that stood in the far corner. "This is our baby," he said.

I stooped down over the crib. The baby's only covering was a ragged strip of toweling. The waxen pallor of her face was accentuated by the black hair above. For a moment I wondered if she had already died. Then her eyes opened and met mine. There was something familiar about the big dark eyes. Could I have seen them before? No—that was impossible.

Mr. Cohen's voice broke in upon my thoughts. "Well, will you take her?"

"Yes, I'll take her," I replied. "Do you have anything to wrap her in?"

Mr. Cohen said something in a language I took to be Yiddish, and the woman on the bed suddenly came to life. Pulling the shawl from her shoulders, she wrapped the baby in it. Out of the crib she took a baby bottle with a few ounces of milk and tucked it into the shawl with the baby. Then she thrust the whole bundle into my arms.

I started toward the door, with Mr. Cohen following. In the doorway I paused for a moment. "You haven't told me the baby's name," I said.

"Her name is Tikva," he said. "That's the Hebrew word for 'hope.' Here, let me write her name down for you."

From one pocket he pulled a pencil, and from another a crumpled piece of paper that looked like a bill. Kneeling down on the floor, he smoothed the paper out against a stone and wrote some words on it. "We sold our table to buy medicine," he said, without looking up from his writing, "but it hasn't done any good!" Then jumping to his feet, he tucked the paper inside the shawl, next to the bottle.

Without further delay I set out on my way back to Miss Ratcliffe's house. The last gleams of daylight were still visible in the sky above, but in the narrow street it was almost dark. The baby gave a few brief whimpers, then was silent. Out in the Jaffa Road the shopkeepers were rapidly closing their shutters. Only a few stragglers remained out in the streets.

By the time I reached Allenby Square, night had fallen and the streets were empty. My eyes picked out the outline of the Old City wall in front of me. I thought back to the first night I had seen it from the taxi with Miss Gustafsson. Then it had appeared remote and forbidding, but now its dark overshadowing mass seemed to offer protection. Instinctively I found myself keeping as close to it as I could.

I had just started the final climb up to Miss Ratcliffe's house when the darkness in front of me was filled with a harsh, drawn-out, blaring sound that echoed and reechoed from the silent houses, sending a tingling shock of fear through every cell of my body. I pressed myself against the side of a house, holding the baby tight in both arms, scarcely daring to breathe. Something was moving down the street toward me. I strained my eyes to catch its outline. Suddenly I let out a long sigh of relief! Picking its way slowly down the center of the street was a solitary donkey!

I waited some minutes to see if there was anybody with the donkey, but no one appeared. When I started to move again, I discovered that my knees had turned to water. With my last ounce of willpower I reached Miss Ratcliffe's house, stumbled down the stone stairs, opened the iron door to my room, and set the baby down on my bed.

With the lamp lit, I lined my wicker trunk with underclothes, placed the baby inside, and covered her with the soft woolen sweater that Mother had sent me for Christmas. Then I took the bottle of olive oil from my closet, tipped out a few drops onto my fingers, and drew them gently across the baby's forehead. "In Your name, Lord Jesus!"

Before dawn the next day I relit the lamp and held it over the trunk where Tikva lay. Gently I placed the back of my hand against her forehead. It was still dry and burning hot. If possible, she looked more frail than ever, with the yellow skin stretched taut over her cheekbones. The light from the lamp caused her to open her eyes for a moment. As they met mine, there came that sense of familiarity. Was it somehow possible I had seen them before?

And then in a rush it all came back to me—the day of prayer in the Pentecostal church in Korsør! Kneeling there, I had felt the presence of God come down over me in a way that was almost tangible. And then I had seen the face of a baby—with the dark eyes gazing up at me out of something that looked like a box. There could be no doubt! It was Tikva whom I had seen, and the "box" was my own wicker trunk!

So all this had really been planned by God—before it actually happened! The realization was awesome. How necessary it was for me to play my role faithfully so that God's purposes could be fully worked out. There were just two of us there in that basement—Tikva and myself—but the drama in which we were taking part was being directed from heaven.

The milk had curdled in the baby bottle. I rinsed it out, filled it with fresh water, and placed it to her lips. A few feeble sucks were all she could manage. I tucked the sweater more tightly around her and then got back into bed to wait for daylight.

As I lay there, I began making a mental list of all the things that I would need as soon as the shops opened: milk, diapers, safety pins, a nightdress, a clean sheet, and, if possible, a second bottle. How far would eighty-six cents go toward all that? And what if something should happen to Tikva while I was out?

My thoughts were interrupted by a sound from the inside staircase. It was the tap-tap of Nijmeh's cane. I got up and opened the door for her, then guided her to my chair.

"Excuse my coming at such an early hour," she said, "but the Lord woke me up before dawn and told me to bring you this." She pressed two dollars into my hand. "It isn't much and I don't know why you should need it just now—but God knows!"

It was a moment before I could speak. "Nijmeh, do you remember that sick baby we talked about yesterday?"

"Of course I remember her. I've been praying for her ever since. Are you going to take her?"

"Not *going* to—I *have* taken her. I went yesterday evening."

"You went last night? After dark? Where is she?"

"In my wicker trunk. But she's very weak."

Taking Nijmeh by the hand, I led her to the trunk. There we knelt down side by side. Gently I placed Nijmeh's hand on Tikva's forehead.

"How her skin burns!" Nijmeh exclaimed.

"I know. If only that fever would break!"

"Miss Christensen, our Lord told us that if two of us would *agree together* about anything for which we ask, it would be done for us. Let us join our faith together this very moment and ask God to break the power of the fever."

With our hands touching each other's on Tikva's head, we prayed aloud by turns, pleading with God to spare her life and to drive out the fever. When it seemed we could pray no more, we were silent for several minutes. Then at a certain moment I knew that my contact with Nijmeh was no longer merely physical. My spirit had touched hers, and together we had touched·God! Nijmeh must have sensed this, too, for she lifted my hand from Tikva and held it in both of hers. "God has heard our prayer," she said.

Leading her back to the chair, I said, "Now I must go and buy the things I need for Tikva. That's why God told you to bring me two dollars. Without that I wouldn't have enough. You stay here and keep guard over Tikva."

I hurried as fast as I could from store to store. I was reluctant to waste time in bargaining, yet I wanted to make my money go as far as possible. I returned to find that Nijmeh had been joined by Miss Ratcliffe and Maria. I went quickly to Tikva. There was no change in her condition.

It was the first time I had seen Miss Ratcliffe visibly excited. "Miss Christensen," she said in a voice even deeper than usual, "Do you mean to say that you went out alone after dark to fetch this baby?"

"It was light when I went out," I tried to defend myself, "but it got dark before I could get back."

"I can only thank God that He preserved your life," she said. "I hope you will never do such a thing again!"

"Yes," I answered, "I hope that, too!"

At this moment Maria broke in. "Look—the baby!"

I stooped down and felt Tikva. She was wringing wet! Her black hair gleamed with moisture, and little beads of perspiration covered her forehead. Suddenly I realized what had happened! "Nijmeh," I cried, "the fever has broken!"

Nijmeh raised her arms in the air and began to praise God in Arabic. "El-hamd il-Allah! El-hamd il-Allah!" she kept repeating. Maria joined her in Arabic and was followed by Miss Ratcliffe in English. As for me, only Danish could express my feelings at that moment, and so the air was filled with praises in three different languages. From that moment I began to believe that Tikva would recover.

By evening I could see indications—slight but significant—that she really was beginning to improve. Her breathing was easier and she was able to keep her eyes open for two or three minutes at a time. When I placed my forefinger inside her hand, she responded by attempting to close her fingers around mine.

The events of the morning reinforced the lesson I had already learned in Marseilles: that prayer was made effective when it climaxed in praise. I decided therefore to surround Tikva with an atmosphere of continuous praise. Part of the time I praised God aloud, in prayer or in song. But even when I was occupied with practical tasks, I kept up an inner flow of praise in my unknown tongue.

On Sunday morning I heard a voice calling from the courtyard, "Miss Christensen! Miss Christensen!" Recognizing Mr. Cohen's voice, I opened the door. He was standing on the opposite side of the courtyard, as far as he could from my door.

"Is she dead yet?" he asked. Again that almost superstitious horror of death!

"No," I replied, "she's not dead—and she's not going to die! Come in and see for yourself!"

"No, no!" he said. "I won't come in. I'll stay out here."

I continued to urge him to see for himself, but he remained standing for some minutes on the far side of the courtyard and then took his leave.

Sunday was the day that I wrote my weekly letter to Mother. Of course, the letter I wrote that afternoon centered around Tikva. I wanted Mother to be the first one in Denmark to know about her. "Pray that I may be allowed to keep her," I concluded.

Both Nijmeh and Maria were nearly as much concerned for Tikva as I was myself. This made my task much easier. If I needed to go out, I could leave one of them in charge of her.

On the first day of 1929 I received a letter from Valborg, enclosing a Christmas card and a money order for eight dollars. In a hastily scribbled note she explained, "I mailed this to you in good time for Christmas, but it was returned to me for additional postage."

Looking back over the last few days, I could only marvel at the accuracy of God's timing. If Valborg's letter with the money had not been delayed, I would have received it before Christmas—and before I took Tikva. As it was, my decision to take her had been based on one thing only, the conviction that it was God's will for me to do so—with no indication that I could look to any human source for support. Only after my commitment was made had God permitted money to come in, first from Nijmeh and now from Valborg.

In the middle of the week I heard Mr. Cohen's voice again, calling from the courtyard. My heart missed a beat. Had he come to take Tikva?

"I've brought you Tikva's crib," he said, setting it down in the courtyard, "just in case you need it!"

"Of course I'm going to need it!" I told him. After he had gone, I added to myself, "But I'm not going to put her back on that stained, ragged mattress!"

The next day I went bargain hunting in the Old City and returned with a new mattress, also a can of white enamel and a paintbrush. Twenty-four hours later I lifted Tikva out of the trunk and placed her proudly on her new mattress in a gleaming white crib. These and other necessary purchases left me with only a little over three dollars.

Yet I was no longer unduly concerned about the exact amount of money that I had. I felt that it was my responsibility to care for Tikva. If I was faithful in that, I could leave the responsibility for money in God's hands. Rather than praying for my needs, I began to thank God continuously for all that He had already provided. Giving thanks did more to strengthen my faith than asking for things.

When I went to open my outside door the next morning, I found that an envelope had been slipped under it. Inside was a single Palestinian pound (about four dollars), but no message of any kind. This was almost frightening! Somebody must have been there in the dark. I tried to think who it might be. Perhaps someone who attended Miss Ratcliffe's services? I had no way of knowing. But, after all, that was not my business! No matter what the channel of supply might be, God was the source.

Another surprise followed quickly. It was a letter from Kristine Sonderby in Korsør, containing a money order for forty-five dollars—also a refill for my calendar for 1929. In her letter she wrote, "Several of the teachers came together on Christmas Day, and we decided to send you this as a belated Christmas present." Most surprising of all was the postscript at the end: "Five dollars of this is from Erna Storm."

Erna Storm!—the very person who had declared that my presence was a disgrace to the whole school! "Surely God can turn even stones into bread," I mused.

In my letter of thanks to Kristine Sonderby I told her about Tikva, and added, "Your message about the shepherd on the calendar is coming true. Jesus has put one of His lambs into my arms."

I had become so used to frugal living that forty-five dollars seemed like a fortune! Keeping out fifteen dollars for immediate needs, I decided to open my own account at Barclays Bank with the rest. As I left the bank, I was closer to dancing than walking!

On my way back to Miss Ratcliffe's house I passed a grocery store that specialized in foods imported from Europe. My eye was caught by some Danish blue cheese in the window. A small piece cost as much as a complete meal of locally produced food. But the temptation to eat some real Danish food was irresistible. I bought a piece of the cheese and some Danish butter to go with it. At my noon meal that day I spread the butter and cheese lavishly on some coarse brown bread. A customer at the Tivoli Restaurant in Copenhagen never enjoyed a meal more!

Slowly but surely, Tikva was gaining ground. However, I was concerned about her color. Her cheeks still had the look of frail parchment, too tightly stretched. I decided that part of her extreme weakness was due to lying all day in the dark, cavernous room where I had found her. She needed fresh air and sunlight.

I set out to look for a baby carriage. Eventually, in a secondhand store in the Jaffa Road, I located one of British manufacture, with high wheels and a long, elegant body. It was far from new, but it was clean and in good condition. The storekeeper was asking twenty dollars. After ten minutes of bargaining I brought him down to twelve.

That evening Miss Ratcliffe came down to see me, with an envelope in her hand. "I just received this today," she said. "It's twelve dollars from an anonymous donor: 'for a Jewish child in need.' I can't think of anyone better qualified to use the money just now than you!"

Once again God's timing took my breath away.

The next day, as I wheeled Tikva out in the carriage, I felt that Jerusalem belonged to me. Was any mother ever prouder or happier than I?

From then on I took Tikva out regularly each day, and her condition began to improve more rapidly. Her cheeks lost their drawn, yellow look, and a hint of color appeared in them. It was not long before I was able to give her small portions of cream of wheat, in addition to her milk.

During our walks I talked to Tikva freely, just as though she understood all I was saying. I also sang to her the gospel choruses I had learned from the Pentecostal people in Korsør. The songs I knew only in Danish, but for the rest of the time I used English. It was obviously more important for her to grow up understanding and speaking English than Danish.

Tikva seemed to enjoy it all as much as I. As long as I would sing or talk to her, she leaned back on her pillow and kept her black eyes fixed upon me in solemn approval. But if I became silent, or my attention was diverted from her, she was restless and fretful, yawning and rubbing her eyes—protesting with every movement, "Why aren't you speaking to me?"

One day, while wheeling Tikva along King George V Avenue, I overheard two couples on the sidewalk speaking Danish. It was the first time I had heard my mother tongue since I had parted from Kitty in Marseilles. I could not resist the temptation to listen to their conversation. They were looking for a certain tourist office. Excusing myself for breaking in, I gave them directions.

"Please forgive me for asking," one of them said, "but is that your little girl? She is so dark and you are so fair!"

"Yes," I answered, "she's my little girl, but I'm not her mother."

My answer provoked further questions, and in the end the four of them insisted on inviting me into a nearby cafe for a cup of coffee "and some good Danish pastry!" Here we sat for an hour while I told them of my background in Denmark and the way in which I had been led to Jerusalem. In turn I learned that the two men were senior officials from the head office of the Danish State Railways in Copenhagen and that they were on a private tour of the Holy Land with their wives.

Before we parted, they took my address, and one of the ladies quietly slipped some money into my hand. "You'll hear from us again," she said.

Out in the street by myself once more, I looked at the money—twenty dollars.

"Tikva," I said, "God is good to us!" The gleam in her black eyes seemed to say that she agreed.

10

MAHANEH YEHUDA

Near the end of January Miss Ratcliffe informed me that the house she occupied had been sold and the new owner intended to take occupation as soon as the current lease expired. "That means we shall all have to be out of here by *Muharram*," she concluded.

"*Muharram?*"

"An annual Muslim festival," she explained. "It falls in early spring. By a tradition carried over from Turkish times, house leases run from Muharram to Muharram. So each spring the streets of Jerusalem are filled with people moving to new homes—and this year you and I will be among them!"

Ten days later Miss Ratcliffe told me that she had signed a lease on a house in Musrara, an area about half a mile north of the Damascus Gate. "I'm afraid this new house doesn't have any kind of separate accommodation that I could rent to you," she added apologetically.

"It's most kind of you to be so concerned," I said. "But perhaps God is showing me that it's time for Tikva and me to find a place of our own."

"I wouldn't count on having Tikva too long," Miss Ratcliffe warned. "If you succeed in nursing her back to full health, her family will quite probably want her back."

I made no comment on this, but Miss Ratcliffe's words disturbed me more that I cared to acknowledge. The prospect of suddenly having to set up house on my own was bad enough. But even worse was the suggestion that Tikva might soon be taken from me. "After all," I told myself, "God brought me here to save her life, and she still needs me."

My daily walks with Tikva in the baby carriage now became house-hunting expeditions. I started by looking in Musrara, hoping to stay close to Miss Ratcliffe. Only when several days of searching in Musrara had yielded no results did I reluctantly begin to explore some other areas further west.

Eventually, in a district called Mahaneh Yehuda, I located a small, two-story house with the upper floor to rent, unfurnished. The house was one of a group of six, clustered together on a barren, sandy patch of ground about a hundred yards north of the Jaffa Road. *Mahaneh Yehuda*, I learned, was Hebrew for "Camp of Judah," which somehow suggested a stronghold of Judaism. I wondered how the residents of such an exclusively Jewish area would react to a Gentile intruder. However, Muharram and moving time was a bare two weeks away, and I dared not delay any longer.

The upper floor consisted merely of two rooms with a door between and an outside staircase. The rent was twelve dollars a month, half again as much as I was paying to Miss Ratcliffe, and I was required to pay one month in advance. I counted the money in my purse—about seven dollars. Hoping I had enough in my bank account to make up the rest, I gave the landlord a first payment of six dollars and promised to come back with the other six dollars within twenty-four hours. On my way back home I stopped at the bank: My balance was less than four dollars. Even with the cash left in my purse, I could not muster the needed six!

That night it took me much longer than usual to get to sleep. If I could not produce the remaining six dollars the next day, I was in danger of forfeiting what I had already deposited.

Eventually I got out of bed and knelt on the hard stone floor. "Lord, if Mahaneh Yehuda is where You want me, I believe You can supply all the money I will need: for the rent, for furniture, for moving..." Automatically I started trying to think where a sum like that could possibly come from, but then I remembered the lessons God had been teaching me. It was my responsibility to pray; it was God's to decide how He would answer my prayer.

The next day there was just one letter in my postbox—from the school in Korsør: "Enclosed please find a refund of medical insurance." The "enclosed" was a banker's draft for $169.35. Pausing at the bank just long enough to deposit my draft and draw out what I needed in cash, I went straight to Mahaneh Yehuda and paid the six-dollar balance for my first month's rent.

In the evening I had supper with Miss Ratcliffe. "Tell me," I said. "Why does God so often keep us waiting till the last minute for the things we need?"

"I've wondered that myself many times," she replied with a smile. "Perhaps one of God's purposes is to teach us the lesson of day-to-day dependence upon

Him. In teaching the Lord's Prayer, Jesus told the disciples, 'Your Father knoweth what things ye have need of, before ye ask him' [Matthew 6:8]. Yet He still taught them to ask—and to ask each day."

For the next two weeks my daily trips with Tikva were devoted to buying furniture, providing me with countless opportunities to develop my skill in bargaining. Returning down the Jaffa Road one day, with a chair balanced across one end of the baby carriage, I ran into Mr. Cohen. He was amazed at the change in Tikva and kept repeating, "She's not the same child! She's not the same child!" In spite of his comments on Tikva's progress, I could not help noticing he never once expressed any thanks to me. Reluctantly, remembering Miss Ratcliffe's prediction, I gave him our future address in Mahaneh Yehuda.

By the end of February there was a miscellaneous pile of furniture and equipment, most of it secondhand, stacked along one wall of my basement room, ready for the move. The day appointed was Thursday, March 7. Miss Ratcliffe and her household were due to move two days later.

I had arranged with an elderly Jew named Jona to come and fetch me with his cart. The cart proved to be some rough planks nailed across two poles, attached to four wobbly wheels. This was drawn by an emaciated black horse. It was hard to say which looked more decrepit—Jona or his horse.

Maria helped me carry my belongings up the stone stairs and get them loaded on the cart. Then she took her place on the sidewalk with Miss Ratcliffe and Nijmeh to bid me farewell. Each of them gave me a warm hug and another to Tikva. Then I placed Tikva in the baby carriage and set off behind Jona and his cart. The last thing I heard was Nijmeh's cracked voice calling after me, "Come and see us soon!"

Jona walked along beside his horse, holding the bridle with one hand. In the other hand he carried a whip, but this he used only as a weapon against flies. Each time the cart passed over a rut or a pothole, everything on it swayed and trembled. Twice my wicker trunk fell off into the road. When this happened, Jona and the horse came to a standstill while I recovered the trunk and put it back on the cart.

When we reached the Jaffa Road, we became part of a confused melee of households, all on the move. The humbler people carried their own belongings, either in boxes and suitcases or in bundles strapped to their backs. Others used handcarts, donkeys, camels, and horse-drawn carts. A very few had their belongings piled on cars or small trucks. The atmosphere was like that of a carnival, with the children running in the street beside their parents.

As we trudged up the Jaffa Road, my eye was drawn once again to the Old City wall on my right. It was strange how my attitude toward those stones had changed. At first I had contrasted them with the trim, bright houses of Korsør, and they had seemed so rugged and remote. But now they stood there like trusted friends, guarding my way for me.

It was about midday when I reached my new home in Mahaneh Yehuda. Jona dumped my possessions on the dusty ground at one end of the building, where the outside staircase gave access to the upper floor. Then he collected his agreed price of four dollars and left me to myself.

My first act was to carry up Tikva's crib and settle her down in it. Then I lugged up the remaining items and put them in place, one by one. The outer room I arranged as a kitchen and dining room, with a space in one corner for the baby carriage. The room beyond it, which was somewhat larger, would be our bedroom and living room.

There was no sanitation or plumbing of any kind in the house. Venturing out to the rear, however, I discovered a common yard with city water piped to a concrete platform in the center. On one side a few sheets of corrugated iron on some poles covered a row of galvanized iron sinks. I saw some women doing their washing in the sinks, while others carried water to their houses in four-gallon drums that had once contained kerosene. On the other side was a row of wooden sheds that served as toilets. These were of the long-drop variety—a row of deep pits in the ground, each surmounted by a wooden box with a circular hole and a lid. This sanitation, like the water supply, was apparently shared among the residents of all six houses on the plot—not to mention myriads of flies.

Returning to my apartment, I observed that the ground-floor room below my living room was fitted out as a grocery store. From inside I heard the familiar sound of people bargaining—partly in Arabic, partly in Yiddish. The other ground-floor room had its door closed and its window shuttered. It was difficult to see who lived inside.

By nine o'clock I was in bed, tired with the day's activities and ready for sleep, when I heard the sound of voices and muffled laughter from the grocery store below me. Then a phonograph started playing the "Song of the Volga

Boatmen," rendered by an all-male choir. In the middle of the song the needle stuck in the groove and continued repeating the same two words over and over—"Yo-oh heave—Yo-oh heave—Yo-oh heave." Finally someone must have moved the needle and the record played through to the end.

"Of all the ridiculous things," I said to myself, "to play the 'Song of the Volga Boatmen' at this time of night—in a grocery store!"

While I was still turning this over in my mind, the phonograph started up again. Could it be? Yes, it was the same song! What was more, the needle stuck in the groove once again, at exactly the same point. The third time an uneasy suspicion attacked my mind. Was someone doing this for my benefit?

After the record finished for the fourth time, there was no room left for doubt. Before moving to Mahaneh Yehuda, I had wondered how an all-Jewish community would react to a Gentile intruder. Now my question was answered. My welcome committee was busy in the grocery store below me!

By midnight I reckoned that I had heard the "Song of the Volga Boatmen" about forty times. Never once did the needle fail to stick in the groove. Sometimes the record continued playing "Yo-oh heave" for two minutes before someone moved the needle forward. Whoever was down there in the grocery store was displaying a zeal worthy of a nobler cause.

Each time the song was repeated, it drove sleep further from me. I had purchased some sterile cotton for Tikva, and I tried stuffing that in my ears—but there was a resonance about those male voices that penetrated even the cotton. Realizing that Tikva was awake, I got up to see to her. She was lying on her back with her eyes wide open, cooing to herself. She was actually enjoying the music! "Tikva," I said, "for once you and I don't agree about things!"

It was past 3:00 AM when sheer exhaustion prevailed and I dropped off into an uneasy slumber with the phonograph still playing.

The next day I quickly realized that I was the center of attention for the whole community living in the six houses. When I went to the toilets or to draw water, the other women broke off their conversation and turned and stared at me. The children snickered openly and pointed me out to each other, making comments in a language that I did not understand. I was reminded of the atmosphere in the schoolyard in Korsør after the news of my baptism had been made public. Only in Korsør, I had the authority derived from my position as a teacher, and I understood the language.

By 4:00 PM all activity in the area between the houses came to a standstill, and I was reminded that the Sabbath was beginning. I retired to my apartment and tried to fix my mind on various things, but inwardly I was struggling against mounting tension. Would the previous night's serenade be repeated? Or had some other form of protest been planned?

I followed the hand on my watch as it ticked off the hours. Nine o'clock came—and passed. Then ten o'clock. But the quietness of the night remained unbroken. Apparently my neighbors had no further welcome in store for me that night. Perhaps they were restrained by respect for the Sabbath. Too tired to speculate further, I heaved a sigh of relief and quickly fell into a deep sleep.

The next morning I washed Tikva's diapers and some of my own underwear and hung them out on the clothesline in the common yard. At noon I went out to collect them and found that each piece had been torn down from the line and trampled into the dust. "Whoever did that should be ashamed of themselves!" I exclaimed. I looked around for some indication of who was responsible. Not a soul was visible, and yet I had the feeling that many pairs of eyes were fastened on me. With as much dignity as I could muster, I gathered up my scattered pieces of washing and made my way back to my apartment.

Sitting down at my table, I tried to regain my composure. I had been prepared for a period of adjustment in Mahaneh Yehuda, and even of loneliness. But what had I done to incur this open hostility from people I had never even spoken to? Either I had made a serious mistake in moving there or there was some new lesson for me to learn that I did not understand. I recalled that Miss Ratcliffe was moving that day to her new house in Musrara. I would go to her service the next morning and see if she had any advice to offer me.

It was about a mile from Mahaneh Yehuda to Miss Ratcliffe's house in Musrara. I set out early on Sunday morning, pushing Tikva ahead of me in the baby carriage. As I left Mahaneh Yehuda behind, my spirit grew lighter, and I found myself singing. In her own way, too, Tikva shared my release, clapping her hands and imitating the sounds that I made.

Nijmeh and Maria greeted us both with delight and insisted on caring for Tikva during the service. At the end I took Miss Ratcliffe aside and told her of the hostile reception I had met with in Mahaneh Yehuda. "I really don't understand why they should treat me like that," I concluded. "I haven't done anything to offend them."

Miss Ratcliffe was silent for a while. Then she said, "The roots of your problem go a long way back into history. First of all, you have to understand the Jewish attitude toward Christianity. For them it is a matter of nationality and cultural inheritance, not of individual faith. In this country, a person is automatically either a Jew, a Muslim, or a Christian."

"But why should they object to Christians?"

"The Jewish answer to that is sad—but for them very convincing. In the Middle Ages the Crusaders, with the cross as their emblem, massacred entire Jewish communities in Europe. Later, when they succeeded in capturing Jerusalem—'liberating' Jerusalem they called it—they shed more blood and committed worse atrocities than any previous conqueror, except perhaps the Romans. Later still, in the ghettos of Europe and Russia, it was Christian priests, carrying crucifixes, who led the mobs in their brutal assaults on the Jewish communities."

"But I wouldn't call people who do such things Christians, much less do them myself!"

"Maybe not—but in the eyes of your neighbors there in Mahaneh Yehuda the very name *Christensen* identifies you with such people. Your presence is a reminder to them of the very thing that many of them came to this land to escape. Besides, you did violate their Sabbath by doing your washing and hanging it out for everyone to see!"

It was my turn to be silent. Guilty by association—for the crimes that had been perpetrated through the centuries against the Jewish people. And certainly I was personally at fault in doing my washing on their holy day. "What would you advise me to do, Miss Ratcliffe? Was it a mistake to move to Mahaneh Yehuda in the first place?"

Miss Ratcliffe reached for her Bible. "Let me answer you with the words of Paul: 'And all things are of God, who hath reconciled us to himself by Jesus Christ, and hath given to us the ministry of reconciliation....Now then we are ambassadors for Christ' [2 Corinthians 5:18, 20]."

"Ambassadors?"

"Don't you see? First God had to reconcile you to Himself. Now He's given you the ministry of reconciliation to the people of Mahaneh Yehuda—to break down the barrier of suspicion and fear that has been built up over the centuries. It's a high calling, Miss Christensen."

For the rest of the day my mind was busy with Miss Ratcliffe's words. I had asked God to show me His purpose for my life, and He had brought me to Jerusalem and given me Tikva to care for. That I did not doubt. But was I now confronted with another part of my task—to be an ambassador for Christ in Mahaneh Yehuda?

"What is an ambassador's responsibility?" I asked myself. Not to change the people to whom he is sent, but to represent the king whom he serves. How unworthy I was to do that! Yet I had asked God to show me my task, and I could not now refuse.

Over the next few days my attitude underwent a change. Reluctance gradually gave way to excitement. I began to see my neighbors in a new light. I was no longer offended by their aloofness, which amounted at times to open rudeness. I accepted it as a challenge. To overcome it, I would have to accept my role as an ambassador and practice diplomacy.

I decided to make my first approach to the lady who kept the grocery store below my living room. I began to buy my groceries from her. Her name was Shoshanna (which I found out was the Hebrew word for "rose"). She was a heavy, cheerful woman in her early forties, with two school-age daughters. She spent her days in the grocery store but went home each evening to an apartment in another district. Having lived for a few years in the United States, she had a fair knowledge of English. She never spoke of her husband, except to mention once that he worked in New York.

Each time I went down to the grocery store, I took Tikva with me. Before long, Shoshanna's curiosity began to get the better of her.

"Is she Jewish?" she said.

"Yes," I replied.

"How old is she?"

"A little over fifteen months."

"Fifteen months!" Shoshanna was incredulous. "Why, she doesn't look half that age! Has she been sick?"

This was the opportunity I had been waiting for. I related my battle to save Tikva's life and to nurse her back to health and strength. The result was just what I had hoped for. The mother instinct in Shoshanna proved too strong for her religious prejudices. From then on she became my ally in the fight for

Tikva. Each time I brought her down to the store, Shoshanna would take her from me and feed her a piece of banana or an orange, talking mother's talk to her in Yiddish all the while. By this time Tikva was strong enough to stand for a few moments on her own, provided she had something firm to hold on to.

Shoshanna's store was the unofficial center of information for the residents of all six houses on the plot. Within two or three weeks all the women had heard the story of Tikva and, as a result, their attitude toward me began to change. Before long they began to greet me with "Shalom." Some would even offer to help me with Tikva while I went to get water or hung out my washing. Of course, I was careful never again to do this on the Sabbath!

In my Old Testament readings I came across the original ordinances for the Sabbath, as given by Moses. One of these was a prohibition against kindling fires. My neighbors in Mahaneh Yehuda applied this to such things as smoking a cigarette or lighting a lamp or a stove. However, I noticed that many of the men would sneak out to the toilets on a Saturday and surreptitiously draw a few quick puffs of a cigarette. If I passed near them at such times, I would cough noisily to give warning of my approach and then ostentatiously look the other way. In this way there developed between us a kind of undeclared alliance.

My diplomacy was yielding good results with the women and the men, but the children were still a problem. They took special pleasure in overturning my garbage can, which stood at the foot of my outside staircase. The leader seemed to be a boy of about twelve, named Ephraim. Here was another challenge to my diplomatic art.

From time to time I heard a man, who appeared to be a relative, speaking to Ephraim in English. I decided to use this as a ploy.

"Ephraim," I said, meeting him one morning at the foot of my staircase, "where did you learn to speak such good English?"

Ephraim grew an inch taller instantly! "My grandfather came from London," he answered.

"Then you're the one to help me with these other children," I continued. "They don't know how to behave at all! Every day they turn over my garbage can."

"I'll stop them, lady. They'll listen to me!" Ephraim spoke with the confidence of a military commander about to give orders to his troops.

That was the end of my trouble with the children, and Ephraim and I soon became good friends. If he met me returning from a walk with Tikva, he would always take one end of the baby carriage and help me carry it up the stairs.

The lady who lived in the room next to Shoshanna's grocery was harder to approach. She was a wizened little creature who always wrapped herself in a woolen shawl, regardless of the temperature. Her name was Vera. She spoke only Polish and Yiddish, with a smattering of Arabic, which made communication between us nearly impossible. From Shoshanna I learned that Vera's main claim to distinction was that her grandfather had been a rabbi. She was a widow living on a meager allowance sent to her by a son in Chicago.

Looking from my window one Friday evening just after sunset, I saw Vera come scurrying across the empty stretch of ground in front of our house, which by that time on a Friday was normally deserted. A few minutes later she was knocking at my door. When I let her in, she walked over to my lamp, which stood lighted on my table, and pointed to it. Then she pointed down toward her room.

"You want my lamp?" I asked.

Vera stared at me in frustration for a moment, then caught me by the sleeve and started to pull me toward the door. Mystified, I let her lead me down the stairs and into her room. Her lamp stood, unlit, in the center of her table. From beside it she picked up a box of matches, pulled out a match, and went through the motions of striking it.

Suddenly I understood! Vera had come home too late to light her lamp before sunset. Now, as a Jewess, she was not permitted to do it because the Sabbath had already begun. But for me, as a Gentile, there was no objection. Quickly I lit the lamp and adjusted the flame. Vera's delight knew no bounds. "Habeebti! Habeebti!" she said, patting my arm with her hand. Habeebti, I knew, was the Arabic for "my darling."

From then on, Vera simply took it for granted that I would come down each Sabbath and light her lamp. In this way she was able to postpone the lighting of the lamp for perhaps half an hour, thus saving a small amount of kerosene, a significant economy for a person on her meager scale of living. Lighting Vera's lamp became an established part of my own Sabbath ritual, while on her side she treated me thereafter as one of her best friends. (In fact, she apparently had no others.) Every time I passed her door or met her getting water, she would call out, "Habeebti!"

One result of my move to Mahaneh Yehuda was that my Arabic teacher was no longer willing to come and give me my lessons. I asked her the reason for this, but her answers were evasive. In the end I asked Miss Ratcliffe if she knew the reason.

"As an Arab, I imagine she's afraid to go to an all-Jewish area."

"But surely no one in Mahaneh Yehuda would harm her?"

"Probably not, but if she were seen going there too often, she would lose favor with her own people. Just at present, both sides are watching each other, but in an atmosphere so charged with tension it would only take a little spark to kindle a big blaze."

To make up for the lack of formal Arabic lessons I went over to Miss Ratcliffe's two or three times a week and practiced talking with Nijmeh. I also attended Miss Ratcliffe's service regularly each Sunday morning. But Mahaneh Yehuda was now my home.

———

In the middle of April I realized that I had been six months in Jerusalem and my visa was due for renewal. With Tikva in the baby carriage, I set out for the Immigration Department, praying earnestly all the way that there would be no difficulty about having my visa renewed. To my relief, the clerk simply stamped my passport with the new visa and handed it back to me.

On my way home I heard a high-pitched voice address me from behind in Swedish: "Miss Christensen, whatever are you doing with a baby carriage?" I turned. It was Miss Gustafsson.

I explained the circumstances in which God had brought Tikva to me.

Clearly Miss Gustafsson was not impressed. "I hope you won't let her take up too much of your time," she commented. "Surely there are more important things to claim your attention than one little baby!"

All the way home I wrestled with Miss Gustafsson's words. She had only voiced a question that I, too, had been struggling with. After all, I was a trained teacher, used to having two hundred pupils through my classes each week. Was it reasonable to devote all my time to one baby?

Tikva had a strange way of reading my thoughts. As I lifted her out of the baby carriage and carried her up the stairs to our apartment, she squeezed my neck with both her arms and pressed her face against my breast. It was almost as though she was saying, "Thank you for caring!"

A week or two later I received a registered letter on the official stationery of the Danish State Railways in Copenhagen. It was from the two Danish couples who had invited me to share coffee and pastry with them on King George V Avenue. "Here in our office," the letter began, "we have formed a special Lydia Circle to help you in your work in Jerusalem. Please use part of this gift to buy something pretty for Tikva."

Enclosed was an international money order for eighty dollars. I celebrated by buying some of Shoshanna's finest Hungarian salami.

By this time I had arranged my own special way of shopping with Shoshanna. I tied a length of cord to a wicker basket and let it down from my window in front of Shoshanna's door. When she saw the basket coming down, she would put her head out the door and ask me what I wanted. As I mentioned each item, she placed it in the basket. Then I raised the basket, emptied it, and let it down a second time with the right amount of money.

At the beginning of May I received a parcel from Mother with a beautiful pink sweater that she had knitted for Tikva. I used some of the money from the Lydia Circle in Copenhagen to buy a matching pink dress and a pair of white baby shoes. The next morning, when I wheeled Tikva out in her new outfit, my neighbors came over to admire her.

I was grateful for the great change in their attitude, but my most intimate companionship was with Tikva herself. My world centered around her. It was very small, yet strangely full. At times I felt almost guilty for being so contented. Was Miss Gustafsson right to reproach me for devoting all my time to one baby? Perhaps I ought to seek some larger sphere of service... Yet the curious peace in my heart seemed to tell me that this was the task God had appointed for me.

On her side, Tikva developed an unusual sensitivity to my every frame of mind. If I was busy with some domestic chore, such as washing or ironing, she would stand in her crib, holding on to the rail and following every movement with her solemn black eyes. When I finished a particularly tiresome job, such as ironing a sheet, she would give an audible sigh of relief, as if to say, "There—that's over!"

More than anything else, however, she enjoyed prayer and praise. One of my furniture bargains that brought hours of joy to both of us was an old-fashioned rocking chair with a cane seat and back. I would take Tikva on my lap and then rock to and fro, praying or singing aloud. No matter how long I might continue, she would lie perfectly still in my arms or else join in with my prayers in her own kind of baby language.

One night in the middle of May I was awakened by an intense, burning pain in my leg. I grabbed my flashlight and shone it on the spot. My ankle was red and swollen. Something must have stung me in the bed! I started searching through my bedding, piece by piece, until I found a tiny, reddish brown bug lurking in a seam of the mattress. Grabbing my brush and comb from the dresser, I squashed the bug between then. A drop of dark fluid oozed out—my own blood.

The next morning I showed Shoshanna the swelling on my ankle. "A bedbug!" she commented. "When the nights get warmer, they come out of the cracks in the floorboards and climb up the legs of the bed. You need to get four small empty cans and put them under the legs of your bed. Then fill the cans with kerosene and the bugs won't be able to climb up the legs."

That night, with each leg of my bed resting in kerosene, I slept soundly again. After several undisturbed nights I was rejoicing in the success of Shoshanna's strategy—only to be awakened once more by the same agonizing burning. Quickly lighting my lamp, I tracked down the bug to the foot of my bed and squashed it there. A telltale drop of blood oozed out.

But how had the bug got into my bed? I glanced around the room. There, behind my bed, another bug was making its way up the wall. Reaching the ceiling, it started crawling toward the center of the room, then suddenly let go and dropped neatly onto the middle of my bed. The next moment I had squashed it between the brush and the comb. This time there was no blood.

The bugs' fiendish ingenuity, thus disclosed, appalled me. There must be myriads more of them hiding in the floor. It was out of the question to sit up every night and intercept them one by one as they dropped onto my bed. Yet I could not count on peaceful sleep until I found a way to deal with them. But how? "I need Your help, Lord," I said.

Almost immediately the story of the plagues in Egypt came to my mind. There had been a succession of unpleasant creatures let loose there: frogs, lice, flies. Yet God had kept them under His control and protected His people from them. Could He not do the same with bedbugs?

I dropped to my knees beside my bed. "Lord," I said, "these bugs are a plague, and I have no way to protect myself against them. I ask You to remove them from me—and not let them come back."

Several weeks passed before I finally realized that God had answered my prayer. From that night on not one bug appeared any more in my room!

———————

By the end of May, Tikva was taking her first steps on her own. Of course I had to take her down to Shoshanna and share this victory with her. Then I wheeled her over in the baby carriage to Miss Ratcliffe's house to show the people there.

Tikva had been slow in learning to walk because of her physical weakness, but her mental development had obviously not been affected. By the time she was able to walk, she was using simple English words such as *milk* or *potty*. But of course my greatest delight was to hear her say, rather slowly and deliberately, "Mama." Her favorite game was one in which I taught her the words for the various parts of the face. I would put my finger on my eye and say, "Eye." Then I would put my finger on her eye and wait for her to repeat, "Eye." When she had learned *eye*, I repeated the game with *nose*, *mouth*, and so on.

One day I had just settled Tikva down for her midday nap when Mr. Cohen appeared without warning at my door. It was the first time he had visited me since I moved to Mahaneh Yehuda. Laying my finger across my lips, I led him through to the room where Tikva lay sleeping in her crib. He gazed down at her for a minute or two. Then I led him back to the kitchen and closed the door.

"How is she?" he asked.

"Wonderfully well," I replied. "Two weeks ago she started walking!"

"That's good." Mr. Cohen paused. He avoided looking me in the face. I could see he had something on his mind. "You see..." He paused again. "Well, the truth is, Hadassa has left me. She's gone to Tel Aviv. I've got to go and find her."

"I'm sorry to hear that," I said.

"I've come to take Tikva back." For the first time his eyes met mine. "If Hadassa knows I have Tikva with me, she'll come back to me. I'm going to take Tikva with me to Tel Aviv."

"Take Tikva?" My throat was suddenly dry. "But you don't understand! She's not strong enough for that. It could endanger her life once more! It was only through prayer..."

"I must take her now," Mr. Cohen broke in. "The bus leaves for Tel Aviv in less than an hour."

"But, Mr. Cohen..." A flood of arguments came to my mind, but the words dried up on my lips. A power stronger than my own will or feelings had simply taken over inside me. To my amazement I heard myself say, "Let me dress her for you."

I went into the bedroom, gathered some of Tikva's clothes together, and packed them into a brown paper sack. Then I lifted her—still half-asleep—from the crib and dressed her in her pink dress and white shoes. She whimpered a little in protest, but a minute later fell asleep again in my arms.

Returning to the kitchen, I placed her in her father's arms. She opened her eyes, looked up into his face, and began to cry. For a moment he seemed embarrassed, and I wondered if he was going to change his mind. Then his eye fell on the baby carriage. "I will need that for her to sleep in," he said.

As Mr. Cohen placed Tikva in the carriage, I filled a bottle with milk and laid it beside her, together with the sack of clothes. Still marveling at my own actions, I helped him lift the carriage down the stairs. At the bottom, Tikva stopped crying for a moment and raised her arms toward me, waiting for me to pick her up. Instead, I turned and ran up the stairs. Taking up a position at my bedroom window, I watched Mr. Cohen push the baby carriage ahead of him until he reached the Jaffa Road and passed out of sight. The last I saw of him was the black yarmulke on the top of his head.

Finally I turned from the window and walked slowly through the empty, hateful apartment. I could not bear to stay there a moment longer. I made my way as fast as I could to Miss Ratcliffe's house and went straight to Nijmeh's room.

"Tikva's father just came and took her," I burst out, "and he's gone to Tel Aviv. I wanted to argue with him, but something inside me took over and wouldn't let me. Oh, Nijmeh, was I wrong to let him have her?"

Nijmeh was silent for a moment. Then she said, "No, you weren't wrong. It was the Holy Spirit who wouldn't let you argue. Remember, no matter how much you love Tikva, God loves her more!"

"But, Nijmeh, she's so frail! Her father can't give her the care she needs. I know God entrusted her to me. I don't understand..."

Nijmeh groped in front of her until she found my hand. "At a time like this," she said, "we don't need to understand. We need to *trust*."

"Pray for me, Nijmeh! I do want to trust—but there's such a tempest inside me!"

For a long while we sat side by side, with Nijmeh's hand on mine. Finally she said, "I want to share with you a lesson that I learned years ago when I lost my sight: *Trusting God is not a feeling; it's a decision.* We can't always change our feelings, but we can exercise our will."

"But how can I stop being concerned for her?"

"You can't. But you can decide with your will to trust her to God—and then seal your decision by declaring it aloud with your voice."

And there in Nijmeh's presence I made my decision: "No matter what happens, I will trust God—for Tikva—for myself—for all that lies ahead!"

11

THE SURRENDER

The week that followed was one of continuing conflict. I tried, by every means I could, to discipline my thoughts and to bring them into subjection to the decision I had made with my will to trust God—regardless of feelings or circumstances. I spent as much time as I could in Bible study and language study, but it was a continual effort to keep my mind focused.

Nights were the worst. My mind was besieged with questions about Tikva. Had Mr. Cohen's wife returned to him, or was he trying to look after Tikva by himself? Was she getting the regular food and fresh air that she needed? I could not banish the picture of her in the baby carriage at the foot of the stairs, with her arms uplifted, waiting for me to pick her up. Twice I awoke in the middle of the night and automatically went to Tikva's crib to attend to her—only to realize that the crib was empty.

When Shoshanna heard that Tikva's father had taken her from me in order to get his wife back, her comment was brief: "Men are all alike—all they think of is themselves!" From Shoshanna the news spread, as usual, to the rest of my neighbors. In various ways they sought to express their sympathy to me. The next Sabbath evening when I went down to Vera to help her with her lamp, she had a present waiting for me, a loaf of caraway bread that she herself had baked.

A week after Mr. Cohen had taken Tikva, I went to the bank and discovered that I had only about eight dollars left in the world. My mind had been so occupied with Tikva that I had given very little thought to money. On looking back, however, I realized that the last money I had received was the gift at the end of April from the Lydia Circle.

One day in the last week of June I let down my basket to Shoshanna and raised it up again with a loaf of bread, some oranges, and some figs. I opened my purse, emptied its contents into the basket, and let it down again. Shoshanna counted the money and called up, "Eight cents more!"

"I don't have any more just now," I called back. "As soon as I get some money, I will pay you." Shoshanna raised no objection, and I drew up the empty basket once again.

How long can a person live on a loaf of bread and some fruit? I eked out my supplies for four or five days, but the moment came when I went to the bread bin and there was nothing in it. I turned it upside down and banged on the bottom, but only a few crumbs came out. I came face-to-face with the simple fact: *I had no food and no money.* I glanced at my calendar—it was Monday, July 1.

"It's a good thing I don't have Tikva with me at a moment like this," I said to myself, and then I wondered, "Perhaps that's why God allowed her to be taken from me!" I looked again at the picture on the calendar. Was that its message for me—a reminder that the Good Shepherd still had His lamb in His arm?

But what was I to do about my own situation? Probably Shoshanna would let me buy from her on credit, but I did not feel this was right. Alternatively I could go to Miss Ratcliffe for help. But, I knew, she had barely enough for her own needs.

The more I considered my situation, the more strongly I felt that God wanted me to look only to Him for an answer. I remembered a phrase that Pastor Rasmussen had used once in Korsør: "Man's extremity is God's appointment." I could not escape the conclusion that God had made an appointment with me, which He was now waiting for me to keep.

In my midday Bible reading I had begun to follow the career of Abraham, from chapter 12 of Genesis onward. I felt closer to Abraham than to any other character of the Old Testament. I still remembered the sermon that Arne Konrad had preached in the Pentecostal church in Korsør. It was Abraham's example that had finally made me willing to give up my position at the school in Korsør. I wanted now to trace the successive steps through which God led him after he had obeyed the initial call to leave his native land.

In chapter 22, I followed Abraham as he obeyed God's commandment to offer up his son Isaac as a living sacrifice. I saw that Abraham had to make a three-day journey with Isaac to Mount Moriah—the place appointed for the sacrifice. I wondered what passed through Abraham's mind on that long journey. What inner questioning and conflict he must have experienced!

God had given Isaac to Abraham by a miracle. He knew fully well how much Abraham loved his son. Yet He was now asking for him back. It was hard to see what purpose God could have in that.

I spent the rest of the day praying and meditating. Over and over I prayed for Tikva—that God would show her father how to care for her. By suppertime I was extremely hungry. I had to fight off pictures of my dining table in Korsør, set for the evening meal. In the end I drank two full glasses of water, and the pangs of hunger subsided.

On Tuesday morning I went, as usual, to the post office, but my box was empty. I started to return home by way of Musrara so that I could talk with Nijmeh, but I felt an inner check. My appointment was with God—and Him alone. Even the best of human counsel or comfort would not suffice.

At midday I returned to Genesis 22. Again I pictured Abraham on his way to Mount Moriah. But this time I did not view him objectively, as another person outside of myself. I had become identified with him. I myself was actually making the journey. Somewhere ahead lay my own "Mount Moriah," the place of my appointment with God.

It was on the *third day* that Abraham came to the mountain. I was now in my second day alone without food. I knew that I, too, would complete my journey on the third day. "Tomorrow," I said to myself, "something will happen."

On Wednesday I went again to the post office, but even before I opened my box, I knew it would be empty. Nothing would change in my outward situation until I had reached "Mount Moriah" and kept my appointment there with God.

Walking back home from the post office under the full glare of the sun, I began to feel dizzy. As I climbed the stairs up to my apartment, my knees were trembling and I had to lean against the wall of the house. Once inside, I cast myself down on the bed and lay there with the room swimming in front of my eyes. Finally I dozed off.

Suddenly I was awake again. I had a strong impression that God Himself was about to speak to me. I lay as still as I could on the bed.

"I want you to give Tikva back to Me!" The room was filled with a voice—and yet I heard nothing audible.

"But, Lord," I replied, "her father has taken her back, and I no longer have her."

"You have allowed her father to take her," the answer came back to me, "but you have never given her to Me. You are still holding on to her with your will. I can only bless that which is freely yielded to Me."

God Himself was in my room. A sense of awe came over me. I felt so small and unworthy. Yet God had deigned to speak with me.

Quietly I slipped from the bed and fell on my knees beside it, with my head bowed. Then I began to pray. The words came slowly—one by one:

Lord, I release Tikva to You. You gave her to me. Now I give her back to You. She is Yours! If she lives or dies—if I see her again or not—she is Yours! Your will be done—not mine!

Slowly there came a great inner calm. I knew, with unshakable certainty, that Tikva was in the hands of God and that His will for her life would be done. No person and no power on earth could prevent that. My love for her had not changed. My heart still ached with longing for her. But through and over it all there was the most perfect peace. The tempest that had raged for three weeks inside me had ceased.

As I made my way to the post office the next morning, I felt as if everything inside me had been washed clean. It was my fourth day without food, but there was no longer any sense of physical weakness. My heart overflowed with a love deeper and purer than I had ever known—love for the children playing in the street, love for the blind beggar on the sidewalk, and above all, love for Jerusalem herself. I remembered the question I had asked myself when I first arrived. Was it really possible to love dust and stones? Now I knew the answer: Yes, it was possible! God had answered my prayer and shared with me a portion of His own love for Jerusalem.

On the steps of the post office I ran into Miss Gustafsson. "Why, it's Miss Christensen!" she said. "I see you no longer have the baby carriage with you."

"No," I replied, "her father came and took the baby back."

"All for the best, Miss Christensen, all for the best! It'll be that much easier for you to go back to Denmark!" The high-pitched laugh that accompanied Miss Gustafsson's words was like a knife thrust into the wound in my heart. "We're all going to have to leave or else be murdered in our beds! I've booked my passage back to Sweden at the end of this month. Probably you could get a passage on the same ship—it's calling at Copenhagen on the way."

"Thank you," I replied as politely as I could, "but I'm not planning to leave."

In my postbox that morning there were two letters, both from Denmark. One was from Mother and I opened it first. Enclosed was a money order for a hundred and twenty dollars. The letter explained her reason for sending the money: "We hear over the radio that they are expecting trouble in Jerusalem between the Arabs and the Jews....Please use this money to buy yourself a ticket on the first ship that is sailing for Europe....I am longing to see you.... Your loving mother."

For a moment I stood almost paralyzed. To the ache in my heart for Tikva was now added the longing to see Mother. Was this check from her God's provision for me? Perhaps God had arranged for me to meet Miss Gustafsson at that very moment so that I might know about the ship that would be sailing to Copenhagen.

After all, I reasoned, Tikva had been taken from me. Indeed, I myself had yielded her into God's hands. No one else in Jerusalem seemed to need me. Should I go home where I was loved and wanted? I could picture the joy with which Mother would receive my letter saying that I was coming home.

I opened the second letter. It, too, was from Denmark and contained an international money order for ten dollars. The only message was, "For your work in Jerusalem." There was no address given and no signature.

I was at a crossroads! Which way was I to take? Should I accept the money from Mother and return home? Or was the other—much smaller— gift God's provision for me to remain in Jerusalem? I did not dare to make my own choice. Standing before my postbox, I bowed my head and closed my eyes. "Lord," I whispered, "show me the way that You have appointed for me. Let it not be my choice, but Yours!"

For several minutes nothing changed. Then a series of vivid scenes began to pass before my eyes. They were the scenes I had witnessed in the streets that morning: the children playing, the blind beggar, the women with their baskets on their heads, the laden animals mingling with the people. Behind it all was the jagged outline of the Old City wall against the cloudless blue sky. As each scene came before me, I felt a response of love—outgoing, overflowing love that God Himself had placed within me.

My question was answered! It was the same answer I had received in Miss Ratcliffe's basement on Christmas Eve. My own plans and feelings were on a human level, fluctuating and changeful. But God's purpose was on another level, and it remained unchanged. *My place was in Jerusalem!*

I walked over to a counter and cashed the ten-dollar money order. Then I quickly wrote a letter to Mother, thanking her for her love and concern, but explaining that I was not ready to leave Jerusalem. I enclosed her money order in the envelope and mailed it back to her.

———————

One morning the following week I awoke earlier than usual with a strong sense of expectancy. Something important was about to happen! I lay in bed for a while trying to imagine what the day might bring—but without success. Eventually I turned to my reading from the New Testament for that day, which began at the eleventh chapter of the epistle to the Hebrews. After the first few verses I was surprised to find myself once again following the story of Abraham. Was there something further about Abraham that God was trying to show me?

The writer of the Hebrews epistle traced Abraham's story in outline, bringing it to its climax with the offering of Isaac on Mount Moriah. But he emphasized something I had not noticed in the Genesis account: Abraham never doubted that God would restore Isaac to him, even if it meant raising him from the dead. Somehow this changed my own perspective.

In my reading from Genesis the previous week, I had felt myself to be one with Abraham in his long, testing journey to make the sacrifice on Mount Moriah. But now I pictured him coming down from the mountain after the test was over. Faith had triumphed! His head erect and his face radiant, he descended the rocky path. By his side walked the child whom he had offered up to God and received back again from God. In his ears there sounded still the promise that had been given him from heaven: "In blessing I will bless thee, and in multiplying I will multiply thy seed as the stars of the heaven" (Genesis 22:17; see Hebrews 6:14).

"Thy seed," I said. "That was Isaac! God not only gave Isaac back—He gave him back multiplied many times over."

The lesson of the story stood out so clearly that I jotted it down in outline at the foot of the page: *First God gives to us—Then we give back to God—Finally God gives back again to us—blessed and multiplied beyond our power to imagine.*

My meditations were interrupted by a loud knocking that summoned me to the door. Standing on the platform at the top of the stairs was a frail little woman in a faded cotton dress, her head covered by a colored scarf.

"Miss Christensen, do you remember me?" she asked in Arabic.

I looked at her carefully. "No," I replied in the same language, "I'm afraid I don't."

"I'm the mother of Tikva!"

I had seen her only as a figure huddled in a shawl in that dark cavernous room.

"Forgive me," I said, thankful for the long hours of language study that now made it possible for me to converse with her. "I remember you now. Please come in!"

"No, I can't stay! But I've come to ask you something. Will you please take Tikva back? She's with her father in Tel Aviv—here is the address." She handed me a slip of paper.

"Then you and your husband are not together?"

"No, Miss Christensen, I can't live with that man! He doesn't provide for me—he leaves me to starve! I went to Tel Aviv by myself to find work, but there was none."

"But, Mrs. Cohen, suppose your husband will not give Tikva back to me?"

"Miss Christensen, you pray!" She clasped her hands together. "I know he will give her back! He must! Otherwise she will die." A moment later she was down the stairs and scurrying across the lot.

I glanced at my watch—nine o'clock! Pausing only to pick up my purse, I set out for the bus station. Half an hour later I was on my way to Tel Aviv. My mind was busy with questions. How could I approach Mr. Cohen? What if he refused to give Tikva up? The more I tried to work things out in advance, the more problems I foresaw. Finally I said, "Lord, I will plan nothing and prepare nothing! I will trust You to give me the right words when I need them!"

From the bus stop in Tel Aviv I made my way to the address that Mrs. Cohen had given me, a distance of about one mile. The lady who answered the door told me, in German, that Mr. Cohen had rented a room from her, but that he was out looking for work. Fortunately I knew enough German to carry on a simple conversation.

"Does he have a baby girl with him?" I asked.

"Yes, he keeps her in the room with him—in a baby carriage," she added.

"May I see her, please? Her mother sent me."

The lady hesitated for a moment, then led me to a room at the back of the house. The baby carriage stood under the window. I ran quickly to it and looked inside. Tikva was wearing the same pink dress I had put on her the day her father took her, but it was faded and stained almost beyond recognition. Her cheeks had lost their color, and there was an open sore on her forehead.

As I leaned down over her, she opened her eyes and looked up at me with a dull, almost unseeing stare. Then a spark of recognition seemed to kindle. She reached up her finger toward me and touched my eye. "Eye," she said in a voice that was little more than a whisper. Then her eyes closed again.

The lady of the house excused herself. I sat down on the only chair in the room and began to pray earnestly, "Lord, give me the words to speak!"

After about forty minutes I heard voices in the hallway. The next moment Mr. Cohen came in. In the doorway he stopped. "Miss Christensen!" he said. "How did you come here?" He looked at me as if I were a ghost.

As I faced him, I felt the same power at work within me that had restrained me from arguing or pleading with him when he came to take Tikva from me. But now words were given to me to speak—charged with an authority far greater than my own.

"Your wife sent me to take Tikva," I said. "Tikva is sick again, and you are not able to care for her. If you keep her here, she will die."

This time it was Mr. Cohen who was unable to speak. He opened his mouth two or three times, but no words came.

"Please help me with the baby carriage," I continued. "I'm going to take her back to Jerusalem with me." I made no attempt to argue or to raise my voice, but the effect of my words upon Mr. Cohen was dramatic. His hands were actually trembling as he took hold of the baby carriage. Together we lifted it out into the street and set out for the bus stop.

At the bus station, Mr. Cohen helped to get the baby carriage fastened to the luggage rack on the roof of the bus while I took my place inside, with Tikva in my arms. As the bus drew out, Mr. Cohen stood waving to me. For the first time, I saw him smile. I realized that he had been delivered from a burden that he was not able to bear.

In my arms on the bus, Tikva snuggled herself as close to me as she could. From time to time she raised her finger to my eye or my nose, but she lacked the strength to say the words. In return, I quietly hummed to her the choruses that she loved best. The companionship between us was deeper than words. My heart overflowed with love for her and with gratitude to God for giving her back to me. Mentally I pictured Abraham walking down from Mount Moriah with Isaac beside him. "I believe I know what he felt," I said to myself.

As I wheeled the baby carriage past Shoshanna's store, she spied us through the open door. "It's Tikva!" she exclaimed. "You've got her back!"

As I told her what had happened, she bent over the baby carriage, talking her baby talk in Yiddish to Tikva. Then she went back into the store and returned with two cans of milk. I began to open my purse, but Shoshanna thrust it away.

"A gift from a Jewish mother to a Jewish baby!"

Back in my apartment I was able to examine Tikva properly. She had lost both weight and strength. I had already seen the sore on her forehead, but I discovered others on her back that were swollen and filled with pus. I would be afraid to treat them without proper medical advice. Altogether, Tikva was desperately frail. But the main thing was that God had given her back to me. He would not fail me!

Next I took stock of my financial position. The ten-dollar gift from the unnamed donor in Denmark was nearly gone. We were already into the second week of July, and I had not yet paid my twelve-dollar rent for the month. I had sent the best of Tikva's clothes with her when her father took her, and in my excitement I had forgotten to ask for them back. I would have to buy new ones in their place. Then there would be the medical expenses...

"I really need a big sum," I said, half to myself and half to God. "At least fifty dollars!" It was at once a statement, a wish, and a prayer.

In the postbox the next morning there was a letter—from Denmark! With excitement I turned it over to read the name of the sender. Erna Storm! My excitement turned to disappointment. What could Erna have to write to me about? True, she had once sent me five dollars through Kristine Sonderby, but a sum like that would not go far to meet my needs that day.

As I read the opening phrases of Erna's letter, my mood changed again—from disappointment to amazement:

Dear Lydia,

I must begin by asking your forgiveness for all the bad things I said about you when you were baptized nearly two years ago. I am afraid that it took me a long while to see how wrong I had been, but God has been good and patient with me.

I cannot tell you all that has happened since you left Korsør, but on Sunday, June 23, I, too, received the precious gift of the Holy Spirit and about a week later I was baptized as a believer by Pastor Rasmussen. Guess where! In Store Bælt!

Of course everybody in the school is talking about me, just as they did about you. But now I can understand how you were able to stay so calm and happy through all of that. This time there will be no need to take my case before any higher authority. That question was settled once and for all when the parliament made the decision in your case.

Kristine Sonderby, Valborg, and I now meet each week to pray for you. The political situation looks grave, but we are claiming for you the promise of Psalm 34:7: "The angel of the Lord encampeth round about them that fear him, and delivereth them."

The enclosed gift is from the three of us.

Yours gratefully,
Erna

I reached into the envelope once more and pulled out a slip of paper. It was a money order—for ninety dollars!

It took me several minutes to realize what had happened. God had not merely sent me the money that I needed, almost double what I had dared to wish for. He had done something much more wonderful—He had answered my prayers for Erna. Could I have believed, when I left Korsør just over nine months ago, that Erna, Kristine, and Valborg would one day be meeting together to pray for me?

12

THE SIEGE

Behind her counter, Shoshanna paused in the act of slicing a piece of salami. When she became excited, she needed both her hands to gesture with.

"Why does it always happen to us Jews?" she said. "In Europe it was the Christians who wouldn't leave us alone—here it's the Muslims! There's been fighting every day this week. Even at the Wailing Wall they have to fight! I tell you, it doesn't look good!"

"Don't you think the British will put a stop to it all?" I said.

"The British!" Shoshanna snorted. "All they can do is appoint commissions! What good will that do for us? If we don't learn to defend ourselves, no one else will do it for us!"

Shoshanna handed me my salami, and at the same time she gave a section of an orange to Tikva, who was standing beside me. A few minutes later I was strolling down the Jaffa Road with Tikva beside me, holding my hand.

A month and a half had passed since I had brought Tikva back from Tel Aviv. The doctor had described her progress in the meanwhile as "phenomenal." "Miraculous!" I had corrected him under my breath. I was now able to take her with me for short walks without the baby carriage. When she got tired, I picked her up and put her on my shoulders. To ride thus, with her legs around my neck and her hands clasped across my forehead, had become her newest game.

I had stopped in front of a shoemaker's store, trying to decide if I could afford a tiny pair of sandals for Tikva, when I became aware of a confused medley of shouts and cries rapidly growing louder. Turning in the direction of the noise, I saw a mass of people streaming up the Jaffa Road toward me. My attention was caught by a group of women in the forefront, with their hair flowing loose over their faces, screaming shrilly and beating on their breasts. At first I thought I had run into a funeral, but the crowd was moving too fast for that.

I caught Tikva up in my arms and stepped quickly off the road into a gap about eighteen inches wide between the shoemaker's store and the store next to it. Keeping as motionless as possible, I watched the people run past. The women were followed by men and boys—Jews, from the yarmulkes on their heads. They were carrying a strange assortment of weapons: axes, crowbars, meat choppers, and even bread knives bound to broomsticks.

After a while the crowd thinned out, but people continued to straggle by in ones and twos—both men and women. A bearded man staggered past, holding a bloodstained handkerchief to his head. Blood was trickling down his face from under the handkerchief and clotting in his beard.

A few minutes later I heard the sound of sobbing. Then a young woman came past, just a few feet from me. Momentarily I glimpsed the limp body of a little boy clasped to her breast—his face deathly white and his head tilted back over her arm. Between sobs the woman was moaning his name over and over: "Ami—Ami—Ami."

Eventually I could see no further signs of movement in the street. Tikva was beginning to fuss. I could not stay indefinitely in that narrow crack between two walls. Should I try to make my way back to Mahaneh Yehuda? I was about to put out my head and survey the scene when I heard a sharp crack and a whining sound somewhere out in the street. Surely that was a bullet! I drew Tikva deeper into our shelter.

After several more minutes without any visible activity, I moved my head forward, inch by inch, until I could see up and down the street in both directions. The first thing that caught my eye was an upturned yarmulke lying in the middle of the road. But for the whole length of the street there was not a person to be seen in either direction...

Picking Tikva up in my arms, I started running as fast as I could up the Jaffa Road toward Mahaneh Yehuda. Tikva put her arms around my neck and hung on with all her strength. Turning off the street into the lot where our little cluster of houses stood, I stopped for a moment in dismay. An uncanny pall of silence hung over everything. Normally the area would have been busy with children playing and women at the washtubs, but now there was no one to be seen. Every door was closed, every window shuttered. I banged on two of them—"Shoshanna! Vera!"—but there was no response.

At the corner of the building I stepped on a small, round object that moved under my foot, almost causing me to fall. I glanced down. It was a bullet! Instinctively I looked all around to see who could have fired it—but there was not a person visible. I climbed my stairs two at a time and burst into my apartment. Pausing just long enough to set Tikva down in her crib, I locked my outside door and pushed the kitchen table hard up against it. Then I closed the shutters across the window of each room and leaned, still panting, against the wall of my bedroom.

When I had recovered my breath, I cautiously parted the shutters over my bedroom window an inch or two and looked out. Mahaneh Yehuda had taken on the air of a besieged city. Along the Jaffa Road, as far as the eye could see, rocks were piled in front of doors and windows, and on the balconies of each house. What was their purpose? To keep out bullets—or to be hurled at anyone who might attack? I could not help reflecting that defenses such as these would be pitifully inadequate if the Arabs carried rifles in any numbers.

After some time, men and women gradually emerged in twos and threes from the houses on either side of the Jaffa Road and began to build a roadblock. The women dug up rocks from the road or from vacant lots. Others filled empty kerosene drums with sand. Then they passed them to the men who stacked them on top of each other across the width of the road. As soon as the barricade was complete, both men and women melted from sight once more.

Still, in my own little cluster of houses there was not a sign of life or movement. The silence was unnerving. Had all my neighbors fled, or were some of them still there barricaded inside their houses, as I myself was?

With the August sun beating down on the roof and scarcely any air circulating, the heat in the apartment soon became a test of endurance. At the same time the closed shutters created an artificial twilight that added greatly to the atmosphere of gloom and isolation.

If we were to be shut up here any length of time, I decided I had better check my supplies. There was enough food on our shelves for a couple of days, if used sparingly. I was particularly grateful for a small can of milk. But when I looked in the earthen pitcher in which I kept water, my heart sank. There were just a few inches of water at the bottom—less than two pints. I had been meaning to go out to the faucet in the common yard and draw a fresh supply as soon as I got back from my walk with Tikva.

Should I go out immediately and fill my pitcher? It would mean going a hundred feet or more across the open yard to the faucet. I had barely framed this question when shooting broke out again, somewhere to the east of us. From time to time I heard the whine of a bullet passing behind the house. It would be madness to expose myself in that open space in daylight. Suppose I were struck by a bullet and could not get back to the apartment again; what would happen to Tikva? I began to blame myself that I was not better prepared. After all, several different people had warned me that trouble was coming.

Apart from the heat and the shortage of water, my greatest problem was lack of information. I would never have believed that a city the size of Jerusalem could—in the middle of the day—be so silent. It was almost a relief each time rifle shots punctuated the silence. I tried in vain to picture what might be going on. "If I ever get out of this alive," I told myself, "my first purchase will be a portable radio!"

When darkness fell, my sense of isolation became total. Even at the best of times Mahaneh Yehuda was poorly lighted. But now there was not a single light to be seen anywhere, either in the street or in the houses, and I did not dare to light my own.

From time to time I went to the window and peered through the crack between the shutters, but I could see only the shadowy outlines of the houses silhouetted against a starlit sky. At one point I thought I could detect the figure of a man in a crouched position running between the houses. A minute or two later I heard the soft pad of footsteps in the sand immediately below my window, and my heart began pounding in my chest. But the steps passed on and silence descended again, broken only by the usual sporadic shots.

About midnight the sky over the Old City was illuminated by a dull red glow that lasted an hour or two, then slowly faded away. Involuntarily I formed a vivid picture of houses on fire and wondered about the fate of the people inside. Eventually I stretched myself out on my bed, fully dressed, and tried to rest—but without much success. All too clearly I recalled the words of Miss Gustafsson on the steps of the post office: "We'll all be murdered in our beds!"

The next morning there was no visible change in the situation. Everywhere the doors were still closed, the windows shuttered, the streets empty. I attended to Tikva as well as I could. There was no question of washing her. I decided the best way to eke out our water was to mix it with milk from the can and give it to her in her bottle. I also drank a few mouthfuls of this mixture myself.

About midday I put Tikva back in her crib for a nap. By this time the sense of isolation was becoming unbearable. Without a radio, without a newspaper, without any contact with my neighbors, I had only one source of information to turn to—the Bible. Sitting at my table, with my Bible closed in front of me, I said, "Lord, if there is something in this Book that will help me to understand what is happening and what part You have for me to play in it all, please show it to me now." Then I flipped my Bible open.

From the page in front of me there leaped to meet my eye two verses in Isaiah that I had already underlined in blue:

I have set watchmen upon thy walls, O Jerusalem, which shall never hold their peace day nor night: ye that make mention of the LORD, keep not silence. And give him no rest, till he establish, and till he make Jerusalem a praise in the earth.   (Isaiah 62:6–7)

Watchmen—on the walls of Jerusalem—which shall never hold their peace.

"That must be a picture of people praying," I thought, "praying with tremendous earnestness and persistence—their prayers all focused on one place—Jerusalem." But why Jerusalem? What was there about this city that made it different from all others? I began to turn the pages of my Bible looking for an answer.

In the next four hours my whole perspective changed. It was like being lifted up into space and looking down upon the world from God's viewpoint. Earth, as I now saw it, had one God-appointed center: Jerusalem. Out from this center, in the divine plan, truth and peace were to flow forth to all lands; to it would return the worship and offerings of all nations. In the fulfillment of this plan lay earth's only hope. Apart from Jerusalem there was no other source of peace.

This gave new meaning to the familiar words of Psalm 122:6: "Pray for the peace of Jerusalem." I no longer saw this merely as a call to pray for one city in a land that was a tiny fraction of the earth's total surface. The outworking of this prayer would bless all lands and all peoples. The peace of the whole world depended upon the peace of Jerusalem.

Why, then, had this very city—more than any other—been afflicted through three millennia with everything that was the opposite of peace: war, massacre, destruction, and oppression? I could find only one explanation: *Jerusalem was the battleground of spiritual powers.*

Some of the passages I read left me with no room to doubt that there were spiritual forces of evil at work in the world—"principalities and powers," Paul called them—deliberately and systematically opposing both the purposes and the people of God. Nowhere on earth was this opposition more intense or more concentrated than at Jerusalem. God's choice of the city as the center of blessing for the world made it also the focus for the opposing forces of evil. In fact, I began to see Jerusalem as the stage upon which this cosmic conflict between good and evil would come to its climax—a climax long foreseen by the prophets, now seemingly close at hand.

That was why the problems of Jerusalem defied all attempts to find a solution on a merely political plane, as the situation all around me at that moment bore testimony. Neither politicians with their conferences nor generals with their armies could solve Jerusalem's problems. The answer must be sought on a higher plane. Spiritual force must be met by spiritual force. There was only one power strong enough to overcome the opposing forces of evil—the power of prayer.

I came back yet once more to Psalm 122: "Pray for the peace of Jerusalem." I sensed a divine emphasis upon that word *pray*. Nothing else would bring peace to Jerusalem but prayer.

"Milk, Mama—milk!" Tikva whimpering in her crib broke in upon my meditations. Finding her cotton dress soaked through with perspiration, I took it off and left her in her diaper. Then I mixed a few ounces of water with a smaller quantity of milk and gave it to her. I was about to take a sip myself but stopped. All that we now had left of fluids was just under a cup of water and about half that quantity of milk. Until I could replenish our supply, I had to save it all for Tikva.

For a while I held her on my lap, trying to comfort her. When she was quiet once again, I put her back in her crib and returned to my Bible. In the excitement of pursuing the new truths that were opening up before me, I forgot my thirst and the sultry gloom of my apartment. Searching out God's purpose for Jerusalem led me on naturally to His purpose for Israel. The two, I discovered, were intertwined and could not be separated. The very prophecies that promised mercy and restoration to Jerusalem promised the same also to Israel. The first could not be fulfilled apart from the second.

And how many promises of restoration for Israel I found! From first to last, the prophetic writings were full of them. How far, I wondered, had these promises already been fulfilled? In the decade since the war of 1914–1918, a steady trickle of Jews had been coming back to their land. But—if I rightly understood what I was reading—this was but a prelude to something far greater. God had actually committed Himself, through His prophets, to regather them as an independent nation in their own land. To this end, He had declared, He would bend all the forces of history.

Like the Old Testament prophets, the apostle Paul, too, reiterated the promise of full restoration: "All Israel shall be saved" (Romans 11:26). He made it very clear that God's plan of restoration for the whole earth included the restoration of Israel and could not be accomplished apart from it. He also reminded the Gentile Christians to whom he was writing that they owed their entire spiritual inheritance to Israel, and he challenged them to repay their debt by mercy: "that through your mercy they [Israel] also may obtain mercy" (Romans 11:31).

"What a strangely warped view we Christians have had all these years," I finally said to myself. "We have acted as though we were sufficient in ourselves, owing nothing to Israel or Jerusalem and needing nothing from them. And yet the truth is that God's plan of peace and blessing for all nations can never come to completion until both Israel and Jerusalem are restored—and He expects us to be His coworkers in bringing this to pass."

Was this indeed what God was now asking of me—to accept my personal responsibility for Jerusalem and to take my place as a "watchman" on the walls, praying day and night for the outworking of God's plan? Could this have been His primary purpose in bringing me all the way from Denmark?

The more I meditated on this, the more vivid it became. In the midst of all the tension around me, there came an inward sense of release. I had the impression that I was coming to the end of a long quest. Just two years ago, listening to Dr. Karlsson in the Pentecostal church in Stockholm, I had first asked God to show me my appointed task in life. Since then, His purpose had been unfolding, stage by stage. He had brought me to Jerusalem. He had given me Tikva to care for. He had placed me in Mahaneh Yehuda as His ambassador. These were forms of service to men. Possibly there would be others added in due time.

But at this point, I realized, God was speaking to me about service on a higher plane—not to men, but to Himself. During this day of siege He had opened my eyes to see, beyond all individual needs and situations, His own unchanging plan for Jerusalem and the whole earth. In the light of what He had now shown me, He was asking me to take my place as a watchman, an intercessor, exercising through prayer the only power that could bring His plan to fulfillment. I had the impression that I would thus become one of a great company of such watchmen, extending back through many centuries, yet all looking forward to the dawn of a new age.

Confronted with this new revelation of God's task for me, I felt, as always, weak and inadequate. Yet I had learned by now that it would be His power upon which I must rely, not my own. I bowed my head over my open Bible. "Lord," I said, choosing my words slowly and carefully with a sense that they were being recorded in heaven, "with Your help—I will take my appointed place—as a watchman on the walls of Jerusalem."

When night came, I gave Tikva all the remaining milk and water. I no longer had any alternative. No matter what the danger, I must slip out when it was darkest and fill our bucket with water.

I lay down on my bed fully dressed and waited for midnight. From time to time I shone my flashlight cautiously on the face of my watch. I had never known the hours to pass so slowly. The silence of the night was still broken by an occasional shot but, so far as I could judge, none came too near our building. Finally, without meaning to, I dozed off.

Waking suddenly, I tried to remember why I was lying fully dressed on top of the bed. Then, with the return of thirst, it all came back—the siege, the shooting, the silent, shuttered houses. I groped for my flashlight and momentarily illumined my watch. It was almost 1:00 AM, and there would never be a better chance to get water!

After making sure that Tikva was asleep, I slowly eased the kitchen table away from the outside door. Then I picked up my bucket, opened the door inch by inch, and stood at the top of the stairs with my ears strained for any sound. Nothing stirred. Tiptoeing down the stairs and across to the sinks, I held my bucket under the faucet and turned it. There was a faint spluttering sound, but no water came. For a moment or two I stood like a person paralyzed, with the bucket held out in one hand and the other hand upon the faucet. Then the truth struck me like a blow—there was no water! Somehow or other in the course of the rioting the supply had been cut off!

My mind refused to consider the implications. Only one thing mattered at that moment. I must get back to the apartment and to Tikva! As quickly and quietly as I had come, I tiptoed back, the empty bucket in my hand. Tikva was still asleep. I lay down once more on the bed and tried to come to grips with the situation. Tikva and I must find our way to water. But where? Only one place came to my mind—Miss Ratcliffe's house. She had her own cistern and was not dependent on water from outside.

I pictured what would be involved. The distance was only a mile, but almost certainly there would be roadblocks along the way. This meant I could not take the baby carriage. I would have to carry Tikva on my shoulders. About halfway to Miss Ratcliffe's I would pass out of a Jewish area into an Arab area. Here would be the point of greatest danger. Both sides would be watching for some sign of movement from the other.

When should I set out? I decided to ask God for a sign. "Lord," I said, "please let Tikva continue sleeping until it is time for us to start. As soon as she wakes up, I will know we have to go."

To my surprise, Tikva slept much longer than usual that morning. While waiting for her to wake up, I cautiously surveyed the scene once more from my window. Still the same silent emptiness! Then a man emerged from a house on the far side of the Jaffa Road, swiftly crossed the street with his body bent below the level of the barricade, and disappeared into an opening between two houses on the opposite side. He carried something in his hand that I could not make out—a stick perhaps—or was it a rifle? Apart from this I could see no other sign of activity.

At about 7:30 AM Tikva woke up. Her first words were, "Milk, Mama!" But of course there was no milk. I lifted her from the crib and put her on my shoulders. Miserable though she was, her face lit up at this. Mama was playing a game again!

Before starting down the stairs, I breathed a quick prayer. "Lord Jesus, protect us!" At that moment I recalled the closing sentence from Erna Storm's letter: "We are claiming for you the promise of Psalm 34:7: '*The angel of the* LORD *encampeth round about them that fear him, and delivereth them.*'" Little had I realized, when reading her letter, how much I was going to need that promise!

Then, with Tikva's legs astride my neck and her hands clasped on my forehead, I set out in the direction of Musrara. The early morning sun was already uncomfortably hot as it shone down on the shuttered houses and the empty streets. More unnerving than the heat was the uncanny silence. Even a dog or a cat would have been a welcome sight. Every hundred yards or so I came to a barricade of rocks and other debris piled across the street. Painfully I half climbed, half scrambled over them, still holding Tikva on my shoulders.

After about half a mile I came to a barricade, two or three feet higher than the rest, that marked the line of division between the Jewish and Arab zones. I began to scramble over, but halfway across, my foot slipped on a loose stone, and with a rush of rubble I slid down to the bottom again, almost losing Tikva from my shoulders. Realizing that my strength was giving out, I set Tikva down on the ground and sat beside her on a rock. By myself, I felt sure, I could climb over somehow. But how to get Tikva over?

Suddenly I had the uncanny impression that I was no longer by myself. Every muscle in my body tensed. Turning quickly, I was confronted by a young man standing in the road a few feet from me. A scream rose to my lips, but before I could utter it, the young man had picked Tikva up and placed her on his shoulders in the same position in which I had been carrying her. Then, without apparent effort, he climbed the barricade. Relieved of the burden of Tikva, I succeeded in scrambling over after him.

As soon as I was over, the young man set off along the road—Tikva still on his shoulders and myself following a few feet behind. Still trying to grasp what was happening, I looked more closely at the young man. He was about six feet tall, wearing a dark suit of European cut. Certainly he was not an Arab. He might be Jewish. Where had he come from? How had he appeared so suddenly at my side?

The thing that surprised me most was Tikva's behavior. Normally, if a stranger tried to pick her up, she would start to cry. But I had not heard one murmur from her since the young man picked her up. She was riding just as contentedly on his shoulders as she would have on mine. Indeed, she seemed to be enjoying herself!

For nearly half a mile the young man strode ahead. He never hesitated as to which road to follow, but took the most direct route to Musrara. Each time we came to a barricade, he climbed it ahead of me, then waited on the other side long enough to make sure that I was safely over. Finally he came to a halt directly in front of Miss Ratcliffe's house, set Tikva down on the street, turned around, and started back along the way by which we had come. During our whole encounter he had not spoken a single word, either of greeting or of parting. In a minute he was out of sight.

Still wondering whether the whole incident was a dream or reality, I took Tikva in my arms, climbed the steps to Miss Ratcliffe's front door, and began to pound on it.

"Who is it? What do you want?" a voice called out in Arabic.

"It's me, Maria! Miss Christensen! Please let me in!"

"Miss Christensen!" Maria gave an audible gasp. Then I heard her calling back into the house, "It's Miss Christensen! She's here at the door!"

A series of sounds followed—heavy furniture being pulled back, a bolt being drawn. Finally, the door opened and Maria took Tikva from my arms.

"Thank God you're safe!" Miss Ratcliffe said behind her. "For two days we've been wondering what had happened to you."

Suddenly I realized that my legs would no longer support me. With my last ounce of determination I reached the sofa and half fell onto it.

"Water, please!" I said. With Tikva still on her arm, Maria ran out and returned a minute later with a glass of water. Nothing I had ever drunk in my life tasted as good.

"However did you get here?" Miss Ratcliffe persisted. "We phoned the police station and asked them to send out a patrol for you, but they told us it was impossible for anyone to get through to Mahaneh Yehuda."

I described the journey and the young man who had come to my aid.

"*El-hamd il-Allah!*" cried Nijmeh, clapping her hands with excitement. "God has answered our prayers! We asked Him to send an angel to protect you, and surely that is what He did!"

13

WATCHMAN ON THE WALLS

Later that day Miss Ratcliffe filled in the background of events for me, as she had pieced it together from the radio accounts. Political and religious demonstrations by both Zionists and Muslims had developed into full-scale rioting. Then, on Friday, August 23, the Muslims had launched attacks on various Jewish communities. That was the day our siege began in Mahaneh Yehuda. So far, the security forces had not been able to bring the situation under control. Preliminary estimates indicated at least two hundred people killed—mostly Jews, but also some Arabs.

"To make matters worse," Miss Ratcliffe added, "the British High Commissioner has been out of the country. But the latest reports say he's on his way back."

For the next three days the situation in the city remained unchanged, with doors closed, windows shuttered, and the streets deserted. A tense, unnatural silence brooded over everything—broken by the now familiar sound of rifle fire. Then on the evening of Thursday, August 29, the radio announced that the High Commissioner had returned. "Perhaps now they'll begin to do something!" Nijmeh commented.

Early the next morning the stillness over the city was broken by a new sound: the sharp repetitive crackle of machine-gun fire.

"Machine guns!" Miss Ratcliffe exclaimed. "That must be the British forces. Neither the Arabs nor the Jews have machine guns."

About midday we heard the sound of vehicles approaching. Cautiously I opened one of the shutters a crack. A British armored car was coming up the road with a soldier manning a machine gun. Behind it came an open police truck with about half a dozen policemen in it, all carrying rifles. The two vehicles proceeded past the house and turned the corner in the direction in which I had come from Mahaneh Yehuda. About five minutes later there came several bursts of machine-gun fire from the same direction. Then silence descended once more. Later in the day we heard distant bursts of firing from various directions.

On Saturday, August 31, the government announced that the situation was under control and gave the residents in each area twenty-four hours to remove the barricades that they had set up. By late afternoon people began to emerge from their houses, and the sound of voices was heard again in the streets. Slowly but surely, life was returning to its normal pattern.

That night I went into Nijmeh's room. "Nijmeh," I began, "there's something I've wanted to ask you about several times—something that happened in Denmark when God first filled me with the Holy Spirit." As accurately as I could, I described my vision of the woman with the jar on her head and the men sitting around her. "Since coming to Jerusalem," I concluded, "I've seen many women dressed like that one and carrying jars on their heads, but I've never seen that very woman."

"Miss Christensen, I'm truly amazed! You've just described part of an Arab wedding. As a girl, I witnessed that identical scene many times."

"But why would God show me a thing like that?"

Nijmeh was silent for a while. Then she said, "For years I asked God to send someone to care for the homeless children of this land—His own land. And now He has sent you to help the people here—the children, the women, perhaps others, too. If you continue to obey Him and follow each step He leads you, I'm sure that one day you'll see that very scene you described."

"But, Nijmeh," I broke in, "I've been here nearly a year now and all I've done is rescue one little child. When I think of what that involved, I'm not sure that I'm equal to taking more children."

"Miss Christensen, I believe that you've been laying a foundation for something more that God has in store for you. And laying the foundation is nearly always the hardest part of any building. Remember, too, that God doesn't teach us the same lessons twice. The lessons you have learned with Tikva, God will not repeat with every other child He sends you."

"You may be right, Nijmeh, but just now I don't feel equal to it."

The next day I decided it was safe to return to Mahaneh Yehuda. Tikva began the journey walking beside me, but ended up—as usual—on my shoulders. All the way, I was wondering about my neighbors. Shoshanna. Vera. Ephraim and his family. Would I find them all safe? I had not realized how much they meant to me.

Looking out through the open door of her store, Shoshanna saw us approaching and ran out to greet us. "Thank God!" she cried. "You're safe! We all thought you had been killed. Where have you been?"

I told her I had stayed in the apartment until the water ran out and then taken Tikva with me to Musrara.

"You walked to Musrara—with Tikva? And no one attacked you?" Shoshanna was incredulous.

"I prayed and asked God to protect me," I explained. "Then when I couldn't manage any longer by myself, God sent a man to help me."

"A man? What kind of man would do that?"

"Shoshanna, could you believe that God would send an..." I hesitated. "An angel—to help me?"

"An angel?" Shoshanna stared at me for a moment. "Could I believe? I tell you what I believe—no one but an angel could have done it!"

At this moment Vera's door opened and she came out, wrapping her shawl around her. She looked even more shriveled than usual. "Habeebti! Habeebti!" she said, patting my arm as she spoke. Then she placed her hands in a position of prayer and looked upward. I understood that she was thanking God for my safe return. Straining her resources of language to the utmost, she continued, "Me—sleep." She pillowed her head on her hands. "Me—sleep—five day—six day—no eat—water." She extended her fingers to indicate a measurement, about a cupful, I gathered.

Meanwhile Shoshanna had taken Tikva inside the store and was peeling a banana for her.

As I saw the unfeigned joy with which my two neighbors welcomed me back, tears came to my eyes. I knew now beyond a doubt that I was accepted. I *belonged*. No longer was I a Gentile intruder. They were my people. I belonged to them, and they belonged to me.

Upstairs in my apartment once more, I looked around at my strangely assorted belongings—the white-painted crib, the English baby carriage, the cane-seated rocking chair, the Primus, the bottles on the shelf. It was like being reunited with old friends. Each item had a history of its own. I recalled the store where I had found it and the time I had spent in bargaining for it.

"It's good to be home!" I said to myself.

The next morning Tikva and I set out on our familiar journey to the post office. The streets were busy with people once again and the stores were open. I walked more slowly than usual, taking time to enjoy the sights and the sounds that I had come to love. In front of a small jewelry store I paused, my attention caught by an elderly Jew inside, bent in an attitude of deep concentration over a stone on which he was working. I was fascinated by the deftness and precision of his movements.

"Think of the time and the care that he devotes to just one stone!" I mused. "Think of the years he has spent in learning his trade!"

My mind went to my own experiences in caring for Tikva. Had that been my apprenticeship? Unconsciously I bowed my head. "Lord, if You have other jewels—here in Jerusalem—that need my care, I am willing."

I felt Tikva tugging at my hand. "Mama—up!" she said. Stooping down I lifted her up onto my shoulders, and we continued our journey to the post office.

I doubted if any mail had gotten through during the riots, but to my delight I found a hastily written air letter from Mother saying,

> The news from Jerusalem is most distressing and I have heard nothing from you for two weeks. Are you safe? Is there anything you need—money, or food? What can I do to help?

That afternoon in the apartment I spread out Mother's letter on my table and read it through again, considering how to answer each question.

Was I safe? Yes—thank God—I was safe! Not merely safe, but well and strong and happy!

Did I need money? I opened my purse. There was about three dollars in it. I had already paid my rent for the month. In the bank I had about six dollars. No—I did not need money.

Did I need food? I scanned my shelves. There was oil and bread, olives, figs, tomatoes, a few eggs, a can of sardines, a can of milk. Sugar and coffee, too. No—I did not need food.

I got out my pad and began to write my letter to Mother. I used several pages to describe my experiences during the riot and my return to Mahaneh Yehuda. Then I wrote,

> You ask what you can do to help. I believe there are some things that you—and every Christian—can do. In the midst of all the fighting God showed me something that has changed my whole outlook. I suddenly came to see that we Christians have a debt that has gone unpaid for many centuries—to Israel and to Jerusalem. It is to them that we owe the Bible, the prophets, the apostles, the Savior Himself. For far too long we have forgotten this debt, but now the time has come for us to begin repaying it—and there are two ways that we can do this.
>
> First, we need to repent of our sins against Israel: at best, our lack of gratitude and concern; at worst, our open contempt and persecution.
>
> Then, out of true love and concern, we must pray as the psalmist tells us, "for the peace of Jerusalem," remembering that peace can only come to Jerusalem as Israel turns back to God. God has shown me that from now on to pray in this way for Jerusalem will be the highest form of service that I can render Him.

Then I took Tikva's hand, spread it out palm downward on the lower half of the page, and traced around the hand and fingers with my pen. Beside the outline I wrote, "Tikva sends her love, too!"

On my way to the post office the next morning with my letter to Mother, I paused to look at the now familiar outline of the Old City walls. What would it be like to stand up there as a watchman, enduring the burning heat of the sun and the silent cold of the night?

"That would be a hard and lonely task," I thought. The walls are so big, the directions from which danger can come so many. But suppose there were many watchmen, a vast company standing shoulder to shoulder... *Lord, help me to take my place as a watchman on the walls!*

EPILOGUE TO THE 30TH ANNIVERSARY EDITION

Almost everyone who reads *Appointment in Jerusalem* comes to the end of the book and is eager to know what happened next. In this Epilogue, you will find out the rest of the story of Lydia's remarkable sojourn in Jerusalem—and beyond.

The Children's Homes

Lydia knew that God had appointed her to work with the homeless children of Jerusalem. She once said, "God had shown me that my work would be among the children. Now, frankly speaking, I thought that I loved the children and that's why I should take them. Later, I came to see that it's the Lord who loves the children, and that's why He gives me the love for them."

Not long after little Tikva became a permanent part of Lydia's household, people started to bring other children to her, one by one. "It was not always easy because you need a lot of wisdom," Lydia said. "Many times, when they'd bring a child, I'd forget to think about the money. I'd say, 'Well, they need help, so let us eat together. If I don't have any more money, what can I do?'"

Because Lydia trusted God to provide for all her needs, it was in a sense very easy for her to take in new children. The children's home soon grew, requiring Lydia to move from place to place to accommodate all of them. She said, "If one room wasn't enough, I took two. If two rooms weren't enough, I had to take three rooms. And that was how the whole thing, in a way, grew little by little, according to my faith." By the time she left Jerusalem, she was living in a house with twenty-one rooms.

Over twenty years, Lydia cared for about seventy children—mostly girls. The majority were Jewish, but there were also Arabs, Armenians, and Europeans. "They were brought in from the street," Lydia remembered, "and I hardly knew who brought them. I remember one case when a man brought a child in, and before I even said that I would take it, he disappeared. That was how the work grew."

The children remained with her for varying periods, according to their needs. However, there were eight girls whom she felt the Lord had given to her as her "own." Six were Jewish, one was Palestinian Arab, and one was English. They were Tikva, Johanne, Magdalene, Elisabeth, Anna, Kirsten, Peninah, and Ruhamma. Almost daily, Lydia walked miles through the streets of Jerusalem, either carrying a child on her shoulders or pushing one or two in a baby carriage in front of her as she went about her daily tasks.

Training the Children

Lydia trained her children to trust God in whatever circumstances they were in. "We had a marvelous time in the home," she said. "For one thing, we had very little money, and when the children grew, I could tell them the situation, we would pray, and the money would come in. I would tell them, 'Now, here God has answered prayer.' In that way, the children were brought into the work from the time they were very, very small. And afterward they became a great help to me. They would be praying, and they were baptized in the Spirit when they were not more than about six years old."

Yet even caring for children became a controversial act in the tense atmosphere of Jerusalem at that time. Some of the Jewish people and their leaders were angry with Lydia because she was taking in Jewish children, and they were becoming Christians. In her straightforward and practical way, Lydia answered those who questioned her, "Well, I surely didn't kidnap them. They were lying in the gutter, in the street, and you didn't do anything. Now they are well, and you would like to have them. But you can't have them because they belong to me now."

In and around Jerusalem, these were years of unrest, strikes, siege, food shortage, and interracial fighting. In caring and providing for her children, Lydia frequently risked her own life. She was not only "Mama" but, for many years, also father, doctor, lawyer, electrician, and carpenter all rolled into one. Her only coworker was an Arab peasant girl, one of many Arab women whom she won to the Lord. With one or more infants always in the home, she scarcely ever enjoyed an uninterrupted night's sleep. At times, when fighting was going on outside and the babies were due for their bottles, she had to crawl on her knees from bed to bed so she wouldn't be hit by any bullets that might come through the windows.

God's Protection

"I can see the room where we lived," Lydia remembered, "and I can see the men running in the street and shooting and killing one another. One time, I had a very vivid dream that I came downstairs and saw blood on the steps, and even in my dream, I had one of the little girls by the hand. Now, God doesn't give revelations so that you should be puffed up and think you're something. But He gives them for some reason. And when I had a revelation, I would just pray, 'God, if such a thing is going to happen, be with me. Be a wall of fire round about me.'

"One morning, I came downstairs, and on the last step was a pool of blood. I heard later that a man had been killed there in the night. And I had one of the girls by the hand. I can still see her little shoes—they were black patent leather shoes—and I can remember how I lifted her over the blood so she wouldn't step in it." Lydia was grateful for God's continued warning and protection. God will alert people to danger and other hazardous circumstances when they "really love the Lord and are praying in one spirit with Him," she said.

God's Provision

Lydia had a difficult time procuring food during those violent times. She had no one to help her, and one day, there was nothing else for her to do but go out into an Arab section of town to try to buy food for the children and herself.

"I'll tell you a little about how God was faithful," she recalled. "I said to the children, 'Be careful not to open the door for anyone, and be praying for me.' It was a summer day; it was very hot, and I was as stout then as I am now. It wasn't easy. I came down to the Damascus Gate, where all the shops are outside on the road, and I went to a place where they were selling flour. When I went in, the first thing the man said to me was, 'Are you a Jewess?' I said, 'I'm not.' He said, 'If you're a Jewess, we'll kill you.'

"I didn't dare say anything more. I stood there praying and thought, 'What will happen?' People were shooting in the streets, but what was most marvelous, if you can imagine it, was that God sent a woman who used to come to the home and help me with the washing. And when she saw me, she became very excited. She said, 'You are very welcome here, and how are you? How are your children?' I stood there and let her talk, and when he heard that I answered her in Arabic, he said, 'Well, you can have the flour.'

"I bought a sack of flour, paid him the price, and said, 'Thank you. Will you bring it to my home?'

"'Bring it to your home? Never!' he said. 'If we go down to where you live, the Jews will kill us, and if you bring a Jew up here, we will kill him.'

"'Well, would you give me my money back?'

"'Oh, no. There is the flour. That's yours. The money is mine.'

Lydia stood there praying silently to God for help, and soon a young Muslim man came along and said, "I'm not afraid. I'll go with you. I've been working for the Jews. I know them a little."

Lydia said, "We got the flour on the donkey and off we went, the man and I, running with the donkey. Sometimes it would stop, and sometimes it would run. That was really a sight. I would like to have seen myself, really! Then, all at once, the donkey stood still. It wouldn't move. And the man started to beat that poor donkey. I said, 'Don't do it; it's just a shame.' And while we were having this argument, the donkey ran off.

"And now I'll tell you something. You may not believe it, but it's true all the same. The donkey went exactly to my home. When I came home, the donkey was just outside my door. Now, people say, 'That couldn't be true.' I say, 'Nevertheless, it is true.' So they say, 'Don't you know that when a donkey has been somewhere one time, it will always go there again?' I say, 'I believe that, but then again wasn't it marvelous that God knew to choose the right donkey for me?' And that is how I have seen God's hand time and time again."

A Breakthrough to the Muslims

"You can understand it was not easy," Lydia said. "We couldn't go outside because people were shooting. The Arabs had plenty of ammunition. They would shoot anything they saw, even a paper bag in the street. They would shoot at a cat. A gun was only a toy in their hands. So we had a very hard time there. Many missionaries were killed at that time, and you would never know when they might kill you.

"One day, a woman came to the door. She had a bundle with her, and I saw immediately that it was a child. She threw herself on the floor and said,

'Let me kiss your hand, and let me kiss your feet.' I said, 'No, don't kiss either my hand or my feet; I know you have a child, and you want something from me.'

"There's something the Eastern people do. They look in your eyes because they want to see if they can see the least bit of tenderness there. And I knew all that, so I kept my eyes averted and turned my head so she couldn't look at me. But she must have seen something because she didn't move. After a little while, that little baby began to cry, and I said, 'Let me help you; let me give you a little milk for her.'

"'Yes, that would be good,' she said.

"So I gave her the milk. After a little while, the child cried again, and I said, 'Would you like the baby to be changed?'

"'Oh, yes, that would be good.'

"She was very clever, much more clever than I. And then we opened that little bundle, and that little baby's skin was like wax." The baby's condition was much like Tikva's had been, and Lydia told the woman, "It's very shameful that you dare treat the baby like that." While Lydia was telling her this, the woman quickly left the house, leaving Lydia standing there with the baby, who, it turned out, was a Muslim child.

"I could not even wash the baby," Lydia said. "I had to pour oil in the sores. When I put her in a little bed, her big black eyes would follow me wherever I would go, as though she was saying, 'Thank you for what you have done for me.' I cannot say how old she was, but she was a very tiny baby. And later on, I learned that her mother had died and that a woman from her village had brought her to me. So, after all, the woman had been very kind in trying to find a home for the baby."

The fact that the baby was Muslim was significant to Lydia's situation. "You can see how marvelous God was because now the Muslims were satisfied," she said. "They wouldn't attack me because they knew I had a Muslim child."

A Ministry to Arab Women

Time went on, and the shooting continued, so that the children couldn't go to school. Normal daily living was becoming very difficult. In addition to this, Lydia was still experiencing opposition from the Jewish community because she had taken in so many Jewish children. She didn't want this to become a bigger problem, so she moved to an Arab neighborhood.

"I thought I'd better go up to a village near Jerusalem called Ramallah," Lydia said. "The Arabs, I must say, were very good to the children. Now, when we speak about the Arabs, there are the Muslims who don't believe in the Lord, but there are also Arabs who believe in the Lord, and many of them are saved. I lived up in that little village for many years, and they were good to me; they were good to the children. We more or less became one big family. You could sit on your doorstep, and people would pass by, and you could speak with them. And there was hardly a person whom I didn't know and wasn't on good terms with and didn't have good fellowship with.

"One day a woman came to me and said, 'I have been a Christian, but I am a backslider. Would you help me and pray to the Lord?' And I prayed with her, and she was baptized in the Holy Ghost. Now, when she spoke in tongues and the other Arab women heard that, they sort of got jealous. They said, 'What she has, we want, also.' I said, 'Well, come along.' So we started. They came from morning until evening. One day I said, 'I have the children, and I must see to them, so I can't have meetings the *whole* day. But we will make certain times that you can come.' And in that way, we got the meetings started.

"So you can see that it was not self-appointed. The Lord led it that way. We had a glorious time. They would come on the dusty roads with their big baskets of bread on their heads. They made the dough at home, and then they went to an oven where they had the dough baked, and they came back with the loaves of bread on their heads. They would hear us praying, and they would come in and say, 'What are you doing here?'

"'Well, we are just praying to God.'

"'We want to pray, also.'

"'Come in,' I said, 'and we will pray.'

"And many times, I have seen that people have gotten saved, given their hearts to the Lord, and been baptized in the Holy Ghost in just one day. And if you know the Scripture, you know there's nothing that says you can't be saved and baptized in the Holy Ghost in one day. Some other things can't be done in a day, but this surely can be done; I've seen it many times.

"Now, things went on like that, God was blessing, and an American missionary came to me and said, 'You shouldn't have that work. We want to have

it. We have sent people up here.' And I said, 'Well, really, I'm not self-appointed. But if you go to the east, I'll go to the west, and if you go to the west,
I'll go to the east.' I felt, 'I don't want to have it out with anyone.' Not all
Americans who come will tell you that, but I thought it was better to be quiet
and have peace. Besides, that man and his wife were some of my good friends,
and to this day, they are my friends."

For the sake of peace, Lydia told the Arab women, "Go over now to that
meeting he's starting. Be good, pray, and don't sit there and think that you
would have had a much better time over with me. Put in everything you have,
pray, and be good."

Lydia remembered, "They went, and I tell you, it was a hard time for me,
very hard, but I was determined not to be embittered. There is nothing so
dangerous for a Christian as to be embittered. Then God cannot bless you; He
cannot get His way with you, so then peace will leave you. Can you see how
foolish it is to be embittered?"

A New Ministry to Soldiers

Lydia didn't realize at the time that God had a new work for her to do, one
that would eventually lead to a very big change in her life.

"I didn't really know how things would go, but I had all the children, and
we had prayer meetings. Then one day—I want you to see how God is wise
and leads things; He knows everything—one day, a soldier came to the home,
and he was gloomy. I thought, 'What shall I do with him?' I gave him a cup of
tea. He was still gloomy, and he wouldn't go, so I asked him, 'Should we pray?'

"He said, 'I don't know what it is to pray. I cannot pray.'

"I said, 'Will you follow me in prayer?'

"Yes, he was willing. It wasn't exactly easy, as a Dane, to pray and let the
Englishman follow the prayer in his own language, but I did it. And then
when I came to the place where I said, '...the blood of Jesus Christ, God's
Son, cleanses from all sin,' his face lit up. He had been burdened for his sins.
He started to praise the Lord, and he even started to sing. I knew what was
coming. It didn't take long before he spoke in tongues.

"Now, after that, he went into Jerusalem and told the other missionaries
that he had been baptized in the Spirit. They could hardly believe it. They
had to test the whole thing out and hear him speak in tongues, and then they

had to believe it. But from that day on, there was hardly one day that I didn't have soldiers come to the home. They were down in the Sudan, they were in different places in Africa, and when they had a furlough, they would come to Jerusalem to spend a few days. The first thing they did was to come up to me in Ramallah because they knew that they would get a blessing. Sometimes, they were baptized in the Spirit before they even opened the door. They expected it, and God met them. So we had a glorious time.

"If I had been stubborn and said I wouldn't let the women go, I couldn't have had the other work because the Arab women are not allowed to be in the same room as men. These women, by and large, were married, and their husbands were in the United States to make money, and they were living more or less by themselves or with their in-laws. So I could not have had both them and the soldiers, and now I had a stream of soldiers. Most of them were Englishmen, and I've had the joy of meeting many of these soldiers in England, and they have become pastors."

A Double Union of Marriage and Service

God was about to broaden Lydia's ministry even further. In 1943, a young soldier named Derek Prince was serving as a hospital attendant with the British forces in the Sudan. He came from a respected British military family, excelled in academics, especially philosophy and languages, and had been elected a fellow of King's College, Cambridge. When World War II broke out, he joined the Royal Army Medical Corps. Although he considered himself an atheist, he started reading the Bible in a continual quest for the meaning of life. Just before being shipped to North Africa, he had a personal encounter with Jesus Christ. His focus in life changed completely, and he started studying the Bible intensely.

A Christian fellow soldier told him, "If you want a real a blessing, there's a little Danish children's home just north of Jerusalem that you should visit." The next time Derek got leave, he spent two weeks in Jerusalem, and a missionary there took him out one afternoon to visit Lydia in her home. He said, "The impression of peace and joy that I felt in the home lingered with me for many months."

In 1944, the army transferred Derek to a medical store near Haifa, in northwestern Israel. The following year, when he was on patrol at his army post, he felt prompted to pray for Lydia and the children. As he did so, the Lord spoke very clearly to him. Derek remembered, "The Holy Spirit gave me a clear, forceful utterance in an unknown tongue. After a brief pause, an interpretation followed in English. It was God speaking to me through my own lips, saying, 'I have joined you together under the same yoke and in the same harness.'" The next time he had the opportunity, he visited Lydia again and said, "I believe the Lord has shown me that we are to work together." Her response was characteristic: "Well, if that's so, He will have to work on both ends of the chain!"

In due course, the Lord did work on "both ends of the chain" as it became clear to them that they were meant to be together as life partners—in marriage as well as ministry. Considering the differences in their ages and their diverse cultural and experiential backgrounds, Derek wondered how such a marriage could succeed. For one thing, he was an only child—and here was a home full of girls ranging from two to eighteen years of age! He said, "I was torn between excitement and fear, but I knew God had spoken. His word to me was confirmed by another Christian who knew nothing about my inner turmoil."

Over the next several months, Lydia and Derek discovered they were falling in love. Their love grew strong and deep, and they were married on February 16, 1946, about a month before Derek received his discharge from the army in Jerusalem. By their marriage, Derek became father to Lydia's eight girls. Only afterward did he come to see the full meaning of the words that the Lord had spoken to him about their being joined together. The "yoke" was marriage and the "harness" was service. In this double union of marriage and co-service, Lydia and Derek would continue happily for the next thirty years.

Lydia and Derek remained in Jerusalem through the period of crisis and fighting that marked the birth of the state of Israel in 1948. On several occasions, it was only the supernatural grace of God that preserved them from death. Twice they had to flee their home in the middle of the night and walk out into the dark streets, to an uncertain future, because of imminent danger to their lives. Lydia said that, even though they had a twenty-one-room house for the children, "we sat in the basement because war was on, and there was shooting. One night, I remember about fifty-one panes of glass were broken by bullets" and the general fighting.

A New Chapter

In late 1948, as the newborn state struggled for survival, Lydia and Derek reluctantly left Jerusalem. They went to England with their eight girls, where Derek's parents lovingly welcomed them.

Derek resigned his fellowship at King's College, and from 1949 through 1956, he pastored a Pentecostal church in the heart of London, conducting five indoor services and three street meetings each week. Lydia reportedly never missed a single service. They saw many people saved, healed, and baptized in the Holy Spirit. Also, their five eldest girls were married during this time.

Lydia's influence on Derek's life and ministry is impossible to calculate. Older and more experienced than he, she willingly stepped back and under-girded him as his ministry developed. She was always seated in the front row, praying for him as he preached, and she participated in the ministry of deliverance and healing. Their strength and unity lay in their shared prayer life and endured for three decades as they lived on three continents under many different pressures and in many different situations.

Expanded Ministry

From 1957 through 1961 Derek held a position as principal of a teacher training college in Kenya, East Africa. Lydia continued working by his side. God still had a purpose for the domestic science skills that she had used so effectively in Denmark, as she undertook the task of introducing home economics to the female African students. She was so successful in this endeavor that she received a special message of appreciation from the Education Department of the government of Kenya. Derek also founded a secondary school on the college campus, from which thousands of young Kenyans have graduated.

In 1958, quite unexpectedly, Lydia and Derek took in a desperately sick African baby girl named Jesika. The little girl was found lying on the floor in a hut, and some women brought her to Lydia and Derek and asked if they could take her. Initially, they said, "No, what we are doing today doesn't fit in with taking children in." Both of them were busy teaching school. Yet, in the past, Lydia had remarked from time to time, "I wish I could have at least one little black baby." In the end God granted her desire. Long after she had given up thoughts of taking in any more children, Jesika became their ninth daughter.

By this time most of their other daughters had completed their educations and were working or starting families of their own. They were spread out in various countries on several continents, prompting one of Lydia's sons-in-law to say to her at one point, "Mama, do you know that the sun never sets over your children? You have them in Australia, you have them in England

and Wales, and you even have them in Singapore; they are all over the whole world."

In 1962 Lydia and Derek traveled as Derek preached in churches throughout Canada, and in 1963 they immigrated with Jesika to the United States, where they quickly became involved in the charismatic movement, which was then in its early stages. After living successively in Minneapolis, Seattle, and Chicago, they settled in Fort Lauderdale and were associated with the development of the body of Christ in that area through the Holy Spirit Teaching Mission, *New Wine* magazine, Christian Growth Ministries, and finally Good News Fellowship. In 1970, they both became U.S. citizens.

Stirred by the tragedy of President John F. Kennedy's assassination, Derek began to teach Americans how to intercede for their nation. He later became one of the founders of Intercessors for America, which has carried this message and ministry throughout the country.

As Derek's teaching tapes circulated, doors opened for him to speak in many parts of the United States. Lydia and Derek stepped out in faith in 1967 into a traveling ministry. That same year, their meetings in New Zealand resulted in an international ministry, Derek Prince Ministries, which has subsequently touched almost every part of the globe. In 1971, Derek Prince Publications opened its offices in Fort Lauderdale, Florida, where Lydia and Derek were then living.

A Trip Back to Israel

Lydia recalled a trip to Israel about that time in which she and Derek were leaders of a tour group. "We had the joy of seeing people we had known twenty years back. When we came to Jerusalem, we saw Americans, Jews, Arabs, and Muslims on the Mount of Olives, all praising the Lord. I remember one evening, after my husband had been speaking, they were just dancing and having a good time. They were rejoicing in the Lord. For us, it meant such a lot because, for years, you couldn't get the [Christian] Jews to meet together. If two Jews were together, one wouldn't depend on the other or believe that he was a Christian, but now we saw it."

One day, the tour group was going to Bethlehem, but Lydia had been there so many times that she really wanted to use the opportunity to see the Arab women in Ramallah whom she had formerly ministered to. She wanted to see "her women," as she called them.

"People told me, 'You won't be able to find your home because things are so changed,'" Lydia remembered. "'The roads are different, and it's getting to be a big city.' I said, 'Well, I'll find it.' So a lady drove us up, and I sort of directed her. I said, 'It must be in that direction, go on that way.' We came to exactly where the house is, and I said, 'Stop, here it is.' As I got out of the car, a young man came by, and he knew me immediately. He said, 'I'm one of your Sunday school boys.'

"I really couldn't remember him, but he knew me well, and he went around quickly and said, '*Em al benad*' is here. *Em al benad* means 'the mother to the girls.' And the women came streaming. Where they came from, I don't know, but they just came. And one said, 'Oh, my beloved, my beloved,' and she kissed me."

So many women came to talk to Lydia that their reunion went on for a long time. "I can't tell you what it did for me," she said. "If we could be born again a second time, I'll say that I was, because I was delighted. Something new came over me, to see these women, who had been baptized twenty years earlier, being kept in the Spirit.

"One woman, especially, said, 'I pray day and night,' and I nearly said, 'I can feel that, and I can see that.' She was so close to the Lord. And the strange thing is that her daughter is in England, and my daughter is living with her. When we were in England, I said to my husband, 'I feel that Jameel [the woman's daughter who was then still in Jerusalem] is not having a good time.' She was not married, and I knew her brothers wouldn't be good to her, so I said, 'Can we do something to get her over here?'"

Derek worked hard, writing to people about the situation, and they were able to bring her to England. "It was not easy because the Arabs and the Jews were still fighting. But we got her to London, and I remember when she came with her little worn-out suitcase that was tied with a piece of wire. But she got work in London and really earned a good living, and she is still there."

This young woman had come to believe that her mother was dead. "As soon as I could," Lydia said, "I wrote to her and said, 'Your mother hasn't died. She is still there, and she is close to the Lord.'"

On the trip to Israel, Lydia was also reacquainted with one of the woman's sons, whom she had known when he was a poor and hungry little boy. She remembered, "He would come from school and have nothing to eat, and he would get a piece of bread and sit on the doorstep and eat." Now an adult, this young man came to Lydia and said, "Would you come home with me? I'll take you in my car." Lydia remarked, "Well, that was something new. A very big, beautiful car came and took me to his home. And he lived in a palace. When I say a palace, I mean a palace. To think about how God has been with that family, that that little boy had become the owner of a beautiful, big home. I went into his home, and when I saw the beautiful, big Persian carpets and the mother praying and being in the Spirit, I can't tell you the joy it gave me."

Homegoing

In June 1973, Lydia suffered what was later diagnosed as a "minor stroke." Derek remembered, "She came to me in my study, unable to speak or to remember anything. As I held her in my arms and prayed for her, speech and memory gradually returned. However, she never totally recovered from the effects of this stroke. A period of severe spiritual, mental, and physical battles followed."

In spite of this setback, Lydia still continued to faithfully travel and minister with Derek, even on long journeys overseas. Derek remembered, "She was an amazingly strong and active woman and continued so almost to her last week on earth. At times she would feel her physical heart failing, but she would always say, 'My flesh and my heart may fail, but God is the strength of my heart and my portion forever' [Psalm 73:26 NASB]. From her I learned the lesson that we must not let the external dictate to the internal. Within the life committed to God, there is an inner source of strength not subject to the weaknesses and fluctuations of our physical body."

In 1973 they made ministry trips to both England and New Zealand. In 1974 they led the tour to Israel and made another trip to England. In 1975 they visited England, Denmark, Sweden, and Jamaica. In Jamaica God confirmed His word with a stream of miraculous healings such as they had never witnessed before.

On their way back from Jamaica, Lydia commented, "That's my last trip overseas." And that was the last time Lydia ever ministered in public with Derek. He said, "It was the climax of thirty years of working together 'under the same yoke and in the same harness.' God surely gave us a glorious finale!"

At the end of August Lydia agreed to have a medical check-up. The diagnosis was serious: congestive heart disease and arteriosclerosis, with resultant chronic lung congestion. Various forms of treatment were only partly successful.

On Friday, October 3, Derek was due to attend a convention in Mississippi but felt an inner check and canceled at the last moment. During the night of Saturday, October 4, Lydia experienced increasingly severe pain and breathlessness. In the early hours of Sunday morning she sat up in bed, raised her hand above her head, and said, "Lord, if Your time has come to take me home, please welcome me—in Jesus' name!"

By 4:00 AM Derek realized that he was no longer capable of looking after Lydia properly by himself. He called two of their daughters who lived close by—Johanne and Magdalene—and together they took Lydia by car to a nearby hospital. She was admitted immediately, in critical condition, to the cardiac care unit. Later in the morning, Derek, Johanne, and Magdalene were joined in the hospital by two other daughters who lived in Fort Lauderdale—Anna and Jesika. From that point on, the five of them stayed continuously by her side.

In spite of her physical sufferings, Lydia's mind remained absolutely clear to the last moment. From time to time she gave very practical, down-to-earth directions as to how they should arrange things after she was gone. At one point she said to Derek, "God told me something in the car on the way to the hospital."

"What was that?" he asked.

"He told me that I should thank Him that I have such a beautiful spirit."

For the rest of the time, Lydia was praying and praising, partly in English, partly in Danish, partly in other tongues. In Danish she frequently repeated, "Tak for blodet!"—"Thank you for the blood!" The weaker her flesh became, the more clearly the strength of her spirit shone forth.

Finally, at 2:25 PM on Sunday, October 5, 1975, Lydia went home to be with her Lord. She was eighty-five.

On Friday, October 10, a beautiful memorial service was held for her in Fort Lauderdale, with about seven hundred in attendance. All nine of Lydia and Derek's daughters were present, two having come especially from Australia and three from England. Also present were two sons-in-law and thirteen grandchildren. The theme was one of triumph throughout, and the service closed with an anointed prophetic utterance, challenging them all to move forward into new blessings that the Lord had in store for them.

At the time of her homegoing, Lydia had thirty grandchildren and eleven great-grandchildren. In her last few weeks she had the joy of welcoming a new great grandson and a new granddaughter.

For nearly three years prior to her death, Derek had been working with Lydia on *Appointment in Jerusalem*. Quite often, when questioned about these experiences, Lydia would reply, "Wait until the book comes!" Two days after her death the first copies of her autobiography arrived. Derek believed that God had ordained Lydia's story not only to be a memorial of Lydia, but also an ongoing extension of her ministry, so that we can say of her, "[She] being dead yet speaketh" (Hebrews 11:4).

The Continued Growth of Derek Prince Ministries

The work that Lydia and Derek had begun continued after her passing. "Upon her death," Derek remembered, "I felt as though part of my insides had been wrenched from me, leaving a naked wound. Mercifully, God gave me grace to release her to Him, and He was able to begin the healing process."

After Lydia's death, Derek rededicated himself to the Lord and told Him that he was willing to remain single for the rest of his life, if that was God's will. Yet within a few years, it became clear that God had other plans. In a sense, He brought Derek full circle to Jerusalem and to another woman with whom he was to share his life and ministry for the next two decades. On a visit to Jerusalem, Derek heard about an American woman who had injured her back and was unable to work. Since Derek had a special gift of faith for the healing of back problems, he went to her home and prayed for her as an act of mercy, but there was no immediate evidence that any miracle had taken place. A few nights later, as he sought the Lord concerning a possible move back to Jerusalem, he had a vision of the way back: steep, uphill, and zigzag, not a straight path.

He understood that this represented the path back to Jerusalem, but he noted with astonishment that there was a woman seated on the ground just where the path started up the hill. He recognized her as the woman he had prayed for a few days earlier. Derek understood God was saying that the way of access to that path was through marriage to the woman. A little over a year later, in October 1978, Derek married Ruth Baker, the single mother of three adopted children. From his marriages to both Lydia and Ruth, Derek became firmly convinced that "God is a matchmaker."

Over the years, Derek Prince Ministries expanded in numerous ways internationally. Derek continued to have a special love for Israel and the Jewish people, saying, as Lydia had, "We owe the Jewish people an enormous debt. Without them, the church would have no patriarchs, no prophets, no apostles, no Bible, and no Savior. My most precious possession in life is my Bible, and I owe it to the Jewish people." Derek awakened Christians throughout the world to their responsibility to Israel and the Jewish people. He viewed intercession as his primary assignment, praying for God to fulfill His Word and to bring salvation to the Middle East—to Jews, Muslims, and nominal Christians.

Ruth Prince went home to be with the Lord on December 29, 1998. She and Derek had been married for twenty years, enjoying a happy and fulfilling life together. Derek continued to be involved in his extensive ministry for another five years even as he experienced declining health. Then, on September 24, 2003, he also went to be with the Lord, passing away in his sleep at his home in Jerusalem at the age of eighty-eight. He left eleven children and an extended family of over one hundred fifty people. Through nearly seven decades of ministry, Derek authored over forty-five books, which have been translated into over sixty languages and distributed throughout the world, and he hosted an international teaching program on radio, which is still being broadcast today. Derek Prince Ministries continues to distribute his work while training missionaries, church leaders, and congregations through twelve worldwide offices.

Lydia's Influence and Legacy

As you can see, "the rest of the story" is still being told. The life and legacy of the intelligent and talented schoolteacher from Denmark who was determined to find and do the will of God is best summarized by the words of those who knew her best. In a tribute to Lydia, Derek once recalled, "All who knew Lydia with any degree of intimacy will agree on one point: *she was unique.* There was only one Lydia Prince! As I look back over the years that we spent together, there are four aspects of her character that stand out most clearly— her honesty, her courage, her loyalty, and her humor. There were two words that never applied to her—she was never boring and never insincere."

Lydia considered her children to be her greatest legacy. While the physical houses of most of the children's homes in Israel no longer exist, she saw her children as "living stones," as the apostle Peter wrote about in 1 Peter 2:5 (NASB), and a number of her children, grandchildren, and great-grandchildren are involved in Christian ministry today. "Don't you think I have something to be thankful for," Lydia once said, "to be a mother to all these children?" She believed strongly in the influence parents have on their children. "I think we need to have real Christian homes. It is in the home that our Christianity shall be seen. I'm sorry to tell you that going to church doesn't interest me nearly as much as seeing that Christ is the ruler in the homes. That He is the head. That we have peace and harmony in our homes. That's where we can hear the voice of the Lord.

"Let us see our homes as real Christian homes, and if we are at peace, the children will be peaceful. I have seen that. I could have ten children near me, and they would be quiet. Why? Because I have a peace with God, and no one will feel the peace of God as a child will. If a mother is nervous, the child gets restless."

After Lydia's passing, Derek had remarked, "As our daughters and I seek to evaluate the many lessons that we learned from Lydia's life, one stands out above all others: her tireless ministry of Spirit-empowered intercession. In his eulogy at the memorial service, Don Basham expressed this very vividly, saying, 'When Lydia prayed, skies split and Satan shuddered.' Now that this ministry has been taken from among us, we are each confronted with a personal challenge concerning our own prayer life."

At one point in the memorial service for Lydia, Proverbs 31:10–31 was read as a scriptural tribute to Lydia. After the reading of this passage from Proverbs, Johanne Hedges paid the following personal tribute on behalf of all Lydia's daughters:

> I really don't think there is a Scripture more fitting than that which has been read right now. Every word in those verses describes Mother. Every single one of them. I remember her saying to me several weeks ago (she really liked to reminisce quite a bit about Israel—Palestine, as she called it), "You know, when I went to Palestine I was a teacher. As soon as I held the first girl in my arms, I became a mother." And there is no doubt about it, she was a mother.

I was talking to my sisters last night, and I said, "What do you think was the most impressive thing about Mother that really sticks in your mind?" Every one of us decided that it was her prayer life. She prayed. That was her whole life—prayer!

I remember very often in the nights when I was a young girl I would wake up and Mother was praying. She prayed food to our house. Sometimes we didn't have any food for breakfast the next day. There were usually about eight or nine of us at home. But in the morning food was there! She prayed for our clothes. We never had plenty but we always had enough. Every morning before we went to school she prayed with us. Several of us remember that at times we would start rushing off to school and realize, "Oh my goodness, we didn't go and say good-bye to Mother and pray!" and we would rush back so that she could bless us before we went to school.

Her whole life was her family. The Lord came first, but after that it was her family. Absolutely. She fought for us in every way like a mother would for her children. I don't believe I could ever find adequate words to say thank you to Mother for what she did for us. I remember when I was a little girl I said to her one day, "Mother, what would have happened to me and my sisters had you not come out to Palestine?" She turned around and said, "But that was appointed. I was coming and you were going to be born, all of you, and I was going to have you. Nothing else could have happened. You are appointed, every one of you, to be my children."

She always had the perfect answer to everything. It was never complicated, just like her life. Simple, down to earth. A few weeks ago she said to me, "Johanne, do you remember the lovely days we used to have in Ramallah?" I said, "Yes, Mother, I do." She said, "Those were blessed days, when you were all home and we could be together and pray and read the Word of God."

Five years ago when Mother was being interviewed for her American citizenship, the gentleman who was interviewing her asked, "If America was involved in war, would you carry arms?" She said, "Of course you really wouldn't ask me to." But then she added, "If it were to protect my children, I would." And I think she would have too! Later on when the gentleman spoke to Derek, he said, "Your wife is a very charming lady." She was just that—charming, beautiful, a mother in every sense of the word. We could never have asked for a better mother.

What Is Your Appointment?

The ministry of intercession for Jerusalem that God impressed upon Lydia continues today. There is an army of intercessors around the world, many affiliated with Derek Prince Ministries, made up of "watchmen on the walls." Lydia believed that we all have our own "appointments" with God to fulfill His purposes for us, and that we are called to pray for God's continued work in Jerusalem and among the Jewish people throughout Israel and the world.

"What you do for the Lord," Lydia said, "He pays back many, many fold. I know that Jesus is alive. And I know He cares for every one of us. He will not disappoint you. You'll be able to seek the Lord, and for any true seeker, He will reveal Himself as He did for me as a *living* reality."

Lydia also offered this encouragement and challenge:

Walk with the Lord, pray to the Lord, give your heart to the Lord, and He will use you. The whole earth needs you. Know that there is work ready for you, that you should walk in it. Then say to yourself, "If I don't do the work, no one else will do it." Because God has appointed you to a certain work, or a certain work to you. So pray to God, and be willing to take up whatever He would have you to be. He may want you to be a witness in your work. He may want you other places. There is not a special mission field. The whole earth is a mission field.

APPENDIX:
A DRAMA IN THREE ACTS

by Derek Prince

It was the summer of 1974—forty-five years after the events related in this book. Lydia and I were looking out across Jerusalem from the Mount of Olives, picking out places where we had lived.

"There's Abu Tor," I said, pointing to a hill across the Valley of Hinnom at the southern end of the Old City, "where you brought Tikva to Miss Ratcliffe's basement."

"Yes," Lydia replied, "and over to the right there is Musrara, and somewhere beyond that must be Mahaneh Yehuda."

"And straight across there," I said, "is the house where we were living the day the State of Israel was born."

We continued reminiscing for a while about Jerusalem and all that it had meant in our lives. Then Lydia, being Lydia, grew impatient with thinking about the past.

"But what about the future?" she said as she often does. "What's going to happen next in Jerusalem?"

There was only one place to find the answer to that. We sat down on a stone wall and I pulled out my pocket Bible. For nearly two hours we turned its pages, pausing frequently to gaze at the city spread out before us, marveling at the special place it had held in God's heart through the centuries.

At last, Lydia turned to me with that determined look I knew so well. "Derek," she said, "for months now you've been making me wrack my brains to remember all sorts of tiny details about things that happened forty-five years ago." It was true: Getting Lydia to dwell for very long on the past had required a certain amount of pressure on my part.

"I'll go on doing it," she continued, "but with a condition. That you also put in the book what we've seen today about the *next* forty-five years."

And so, to keep my side of the bargain, I have....

———

In the unfolding revelation of God to man, Jerusalem fulfills a double function. It provides both the stage upon which truth is enacted and the center from which it is disseminated.

We can think of this revelation as a drama in three acts, spanning three millennia, of which God Himself is the Director. Each act has its special theme and each is set in Jerusalem.

For Act I, we go back to the days of David and Solomon—the beginning of Jerusalem's history as a city of importance. The theme of Act I is *the blessedness of a nation united under God.* The climax of the revelation is Solomon's temple, with its unimaginable splendor, set in the midst of a people enjoying peace, well-being, and abundance without parallel in human history.

Yet God's purpose in sending such prosperity—as in all His dealings with the Jews—was not for their sakes alone. He designed that the testimony of this blessedness, and the reason for it, should go forth from Jerusalem to all nations. In making preparation for the building of the temple, David said, "The house that is to be builded for the LORD must be exceeding magnifical, of fame and of glory throughout all countries" (1 Chronicles 22:5). At the apex of Solomon's reign this purpose was fulfilled. Royal visitors from all lands, the Queen of Sheba among them, came to Jerusalem to marvel at the glory of the temple, the wealth and the wisdom of Solomon, and the prosperity of all Israel.

However, the glory of Solomon's kingdom was short-lived. Upon his death, disobedience and division undermined the whole structure. The northern part of this divided kingdom, known as *Israel,* was uprooted by Assyria and scattered among the surrounding nations. Later, the southern part, known as *Judah,* with Jerusalem as its capital, was defeated by Babylon. Jerusalem and the glorious temple were destroyed; Judah was removed to exile in Babylon.

In due course a remnant of Judah came back to reoccupy Jerusalem and the surrounding territory. For the next five centuries the Jewish state that was thus restored struggled along in the shadow of various pagan empires, culminating with Rome. And the stage is set for Act II....

The theme of Act II is *reconciliation—between God and man, between God's love and God's justice*. Speaking as a Father to children who had turned away, divine Love called, "Come back!" But speaking as a Judge, divine Justice declared, "You are guilty; you are not fit to come."

On the hill called Golgotha, just outside the walls of Jerusalem, reconciliation was accomplished. Justice was satisfied once and for all by the atoning death of God's own sinless Son, fulfilling Isaiah's prophecy: "All we like sheep have gone astray; we have turned every one to his own way; and the LORD hath laid on him the iniquity of us all" (Isaiah 53:6). Then Love was able to make the offer of full and final pardon, expressed also by Isaiah: "Though your sins be as scarlet, they shall be as white as snow; though they be red like crimson, they shall be as wool" (Isaiah 1:18).

Once again, Jerusalem was to be the center from which the testimony of divine truth—this time the fact of reconciliation—should go forth. Speaking to His disciples after His resurrection, Jesus explained that His death had fulfilled the prophecies of Scripture and opened the way for the message of pardon and peace to be proclaimed to all nations: "Thus it is written, and thus it behoved Christ to suffer, and to rise from the dead the third day: and that repentance and remission of sins should be preached in his name among all nations, beginning at Jerusalem" (Luke 24:46–47). He also promised to endue His disciples with the supernatural power of the Holy Spirit to make their testimony effective: "But ye shall receive power, after that the Holy Ghost is come upon you: and ye shall be witnesses unto me both in Jerusalem, and in all Judaea, and in Samaria, and unto the uttermost part of the earth" (Acts 1:8).

From Jerusalem as its center the message of reconciliation was to go forth in an ever expanding circle—to Judea, to Samaria, and finally to the ends of the earth. For nineteen centuries this has been the central thrust of Jesus' disciples.

At the close of the nineteenth century, God began to set the stage for Act III. The theme this time is *the government of the nations*. The issue is stated by David: "For the kingdom is the LORD's: and he is the governor among the nations" (Psalm 22:28). The God of Israel has declared that His authority extends over all nations.

Furthermore, He has appointed a King of His own choosing, of whom He has said, "Also I will make him my firstborn, higher than the kings of the earth" (Psalm 89:27). In the face of earth's opposition and rejection, He has declared, "Yet have I set my king upon my holy hill of Zion" (Psalm 2:6). To earth's rulers He has given solemn warning that He requires their submission to this King whom He has chosen: "Now therefore, O kings, show discernment; take warning, O judges of the earth....Do homage to the Son, lest He become angry, and you perish in the way, for His wrath may soon be kindled" (Psalm 2:10, 12 NASB).

By the end of Act III God will have vindicated His authority and established His King and His kingdom over all the earth.

The stage was set for Act III by a decisive intervention of God in history: the regathering of the Jews in their own land. On May 14, 1948, after half a century of struggle, the modern State of Israel was born. Of the countless prophecies in Scripture that refer to the close of the present age, all without exception assume one thing: the presence of Israel as a nation in their own land. Until Israel was thus restored as a nation, none of these prophecies could be fulfilled. Now the way is open for the fulfillment of them all.

Out of all these prophetic visions of the end time, one of the most complete is found in the last three chapters of Zechariah—12 through 14. We will therefore use these three chapters as a frame of reference to make a phase-by-phase outline of the main events that are yet to take place in Jerusalem.[2]

In the opening verse the Lord gives three reasons why He is able both to predict and to control with perfect accuracy the events that are to follow. It is He who "stretcheth forth the heavens," who "layeth the foundation of the earth," who "formeth the spirit of man within him" (12:1). From the height of heaven to the depth of earth, the Lord is in complete control of the physical universe. In addition, He knows and controls "the spirit of man"—the innermost attitudes, motives, and purposes of every man on earth. Therefore His predictions are infallible.

Viewing Jerusalem as the stage set for Act III of the divine drama, let us divide up the prophetic vision that now follows into nine successive "scenes,"

2. In connection with each event there is provided in parentheses the chapter and verse of Zechariah.

each representing a phase of the unfolding vision. Some scenes may partially overlap; between others there may be a considerable interval.

Scene 1:
The Arab Reaction

> Behold, I am going to make Jerusalem a cup that causes reeling to all the peoples around; and when the siege is against Jerusalem, it will also be against Judah. (12:2 NASB)

Here is the first, immediate outcome of the formation of the State of Israel: a violent reaction by "all the peoples around," resulting in a siege directed against both Jerusalem and Judah (the Jewish people). Who are all the peoples around the State of Israel? Lebanon, Syria, Iraq, Jordan, Arabia, Egypt.

Clearly this first phase of the prophecy has already been fulfilled. As soon as the State of Israel came into being, all these nations immediately declared war on it and set out to annihilate it. For two months, Jewish Jerusalem was besieged and was almost forced to capitulate through starvation. Upon this siege hung the destiny of all Judah (the Jewish people in Israel). Had Jewish Jerusalem fallen, the State of Israel would never have survived.

Scene 2:
The Heavy Stone

> And it will come about in that day that I will make Jerusalem a heavy stone for all the peoples; all who lift it will be severely injured.
> (12:3 NASB)

The scope of the prophecy is extending. Now it speaks of *all the peoples*— not merely all those around the State of Israel. All peoples of the earth are to become involved with the problem of Jerusalem, yet none will be able to solve it.

In a measure this, too, has already happened. In 1947–1948, Great Britain tried to lift the stone, but was "severely injured." (How significant it is that the disintegration of the British Empire can be traced back to this very point in history!) When Britain laid the stone down, Count Bernadotte of Sweden sought to intervene as a mediator—but was assassinated. The stone was then handed over to the United Nations (representing "all the peoples") and has become the most intransigent issue in international politics.

God has issued a warning to any nation, any government, any politician who would seek to impose a merely human solution on Jerusalem. All who attempt this will be "severely injured."

Scene 3:
All Nations against Jerusalem

> And all the nations of the earth will be gathered against it [Jerusalem]. (12:3 NASB)

At the time of this writing, this has not yet happened. But the possibility that it could happen is by no means remote. Indeed, with the international oil crisis, a conceivable rationale for such a universal *gathering* is provided—a crisis unimaginable in the days of Zechariah or in fact until the advent of the internal combustion engine in the twentieth century.

In 1947, when the United Nations first voted to bring into being the State of Israel, they also adopted a resolution to put the city of Jerusalem under international control. This resolution has never been implemented; but neither has it been rescinded. Suppose that the United Nations were to revive this resolution and then demand that Israel hand over to them, as the international authority, the control of Jerusalem. And suppose that Israel should refuse to do this. What then? If the United Nations should gather an international army to enforce its decision, against the resistance of Israel, the result would be just what Zechariah has predicted.

Of course, this is only one of various possible ways in which this final, universal attack against Jerusalem could come about. The permutations and combinations of international politics are so intricate that only the infinite wisdom of God Himself can foresee with absolute certainty the course that events will follow. But at this point there lurks in the wings, waiting his cue to appear on stage, the sinister figure of a false messiah. Zechariah calls him "the worthless shepherd" (11:17 NASB). The New Testament writers call him "the man of lawlessness..., the son of destruction" (2 Thessalonians 2:3 NASB), "the antichrist" (1 John 2:22 NASB), and the "beast" (Revelation 13:1–4). (This last word means specifically a fierce, wild beast.)

It is equally difficult to predict the precise role that this antichrist will play in this phase of the drama. A man of unique intelligence and personal charisma, he will rise, through strange and dramatic events, to a position of dominance in world politics. With his uncanny ability to manipulate men and nations, he will negotiate some kind of treaty with Israel, which will enable them to build a national temple in Jerusalem. (See Daniel 9:27.) This will gain him overwhelming favor in the eyes of millions of Jews. In fact, it will be sufficient to cause many of them to acknowledge him as their messiah—although this identification will have no basis in Scripture.

Before the treaty with Israel has run its course, the treacherous deception of this antichrist will be laid bare. Breaking his word to Israel, he will demand that he himself take his place in this temple and be worshipped there as God. (See 2 Thessalonians 2:3–4; Revelation 13:4, 8.) Every sincere Jew will totally reject this blasphemous demand. In revenge, antichrist will turn against the whole Jewish nation with a ferocity that will fully justify the title of "wild beast," and he will use his worldwide influence to stir up war against the State of Israel and persecution against Jews in all nations.

Without attempting to unravel all the subtleties and deceptions of antichrist's diplomacy, we move on to its final outcome, which, as we have already seen, is clearly stated: "All the nations of the earth will be gathered against it [Jerusalem]."

The defenders of Jerusalem will eventually be brought to the verge of total disaster: "The city will be captured, the houses plundered, the women ravished, and half of the city exiled" (14:2 NASB). Indeed, grim disaster will confront Israel throughout the whole land. Two out of every three Jews in the land will be killed. But the remaining third, spared by divine mercy, will emerge to acknowledge the Lord as their Savior and Deliverer. (See chapter 13, verses 8–9.)

This will mark the climax of the period called by Jeremiah "the time of Jacob's trouble" (Jeremiah 30:7). The angel Gabriel told Daniel, concerning this period, "There shall be a time of trouble, such as never was since there was a nation [of Israel] even to that same time" (Daniel 12:1).

However, both Jeremiah and Daniel promised Israel ultimate deliverance. Jeremiah said, "But he [Jacob] shall be saved out of it" (Jeremiah 30:7). Gabriel told Daniel, "And at that time thy people shall be delivered, every one that shall be found written in the book" (Daniel 12:1). Those who are "written in the book" are those foreknown and foreordained by God, corresponding to the one-third remnant of Zechariah.

Scene 4:
God Intervenes

> Then shall the Lord go forth, and fight against those nations, as when he fought in the day of battle.   (14:3)

At this point something will take place that is almost unthinkable to modern, sophisticated man. When all hope is gone for Israel's survival as a nation, God Himself will intervene. The purpose of His intervention will be twofold: to bring judgment on the nations attacking Jerusalem and to show mercy upon Israel. (See chapter 12, verses 9–10; chapter 14, verse 3.)

This intervention of God against the army besieging Jerusalem will not be "military" in the normal sense. It will be a supernatural plague, affecting both the minds and the bodies of the attacking forces. Ultimately these will turn in total confusion against one another and will bring about their own destruction. (See chapter 12, verse 4; chapter 14, verses 12–15.)

At the same time the Lord will also move supernaturally by His Holy Spirit upon the hearts of Israel, revealing Himself to them as the One whom they have rejected and crucified:

> And I will pour out on the house of David and on the inhabitants of Jerusalem, the Spirit of grace and of supplication, so that they will look on Me whom they have pierced; and they will mourn for Him, as one mourns for an only son, and they will weep bitterly over Him, like the bitter weeping over a first-born.   (12:10 NASB)

The result will be a time of deep mourning and repentance for all who survive in Israel, such as the nation has never yet known. (See chapter 12, verses 12–14.)

Scene 5:
The King Appears

> And in that day His feet will stand on the Mount of Olives, which is in front of Jerusalem on the east....Then the Lord, my God, will come, and all the holy ones with Him!   (14:4–5 NASB)

Apparently, up to this point, the Lord's intervention—both against the attacking nations and on behalf of Israel—will be achieved by spiritual power. But, at some moment never exactly revealed, the most dramatic event in all history will take place. Accompanied by innumerable hosts, both of angels and of resurrected believers, Jesus Himself will descend from heaven and His feet will light upon the Mount of Olives.

God will thus redeem the promise given by the angels to the disciples at the time when Jesus ascended to heaven: "This same Jesus, which is taken up from you into heaven, shall so come in like manner as ye have seen him go into heaven" (Acts 1:11). He went up in a cloud; He will descend in a cloud. He went from the Mount of Olives; He will return to the Mount of Olives.

Scene 6:
Earthquake and Upheaval

> And the Mount of Olives will be split in its middle from east to west
> by a very large valley, so that half of the mountain will move toward
> the north and the other half toward the south.   (14:4 NASB)

As a result of the Lord's descent on the Mount of Olives, tremendous geological changes will take place in the whole area. An earthquake will split the Mount of Olives in two, separating the northern part (Mount Scopus) from the southern part (the Mount of Olives proper). The whole of Jerusalem will be lifted up and leveled off, becoming the dominating mountain height in this area. (See chapter 14, verse 10.) This agrees with the prophecy given both in Isaiah and in Micah: "In the last days, the mountain of the house of the LORD will be established as the chief of the mountains, and will be raised above the hills" (Isaiah 2:2 NASB; see also Micah 4:1 NASB).

Meteorological changes will also occur that will make the day that these events take place unlike any other day in earth's history:

> And it will come about in that day that there will be no light; the
> luminaries will dwindle. For it will be a unique day which is known
> to the LORD, neither day nor night, but it will come about that at
> evening time there will be light.   (14:6–7 NASB)

Through all the centuries of its history, Jerusalem has never had an adequate water supply of its own. But as a result of these geological upheavals,

Jerusalem will become for the first time a source of water. Artesian fountains will be opened there and will flow forth in rivers to the east and to the west. (See chapter 14, verse 8.) To the east a river will flow through the valley formed by the earthquake in the Mount of Olives, descending through the Judean wilderness to the Dead Sea. This river will bring life and fruitfulness wherever it flows. It is described in detail in Ezekiel 47:1–12.

Scene 7:
"In the House of My Friends"

> And one shall say unto him, What are these wounds in thine hands?
> Then he shall answer, Those with which I was wounded in the house
> of my friends.
> (13:6)

After His personal descent to earth, the Lord will enter into intimate fellowship with the survivors in Israel. He will make Himself known to them, in the full reality of His humanity, as their Shepherd who laid down His life for His sheep. (See chapter 13, verse 7.) Beholding with wondering awe the marks of His crucifixion, they will ask, "What are these wounds in thine hands?" He will reply, "Those with which I was wounded in the house of my friends" (13:6).

There is a special graciousness in the Hebrew word here translated "my friends." It means not "those whom I love," but "those who love me." After two millennia of estrangement and rejection, the Lord assures His people that He sees the love in their hearts for Himself.

Scene 8:
Cleansing and Renewal

> In that day a fountain will be opened for the house of David and for
> the inhabitants of Jerusalem, for sin and for impurity.   (13:1 NASB)

In addition to the geological changes, there will be a period of spiritual cleansing and renewal for the land and its people. All forms of idolatry and religious deception will be banished. Thereafter, anyone seeking to practice such things will be put to death. (See chapter 13, verses 2–5.)

Out of these purging processes Jerusalem will emerge as indeed "the holy city"—not merely in name, but also in reality. The long-standing distinction between *sacred* and *profane*—or between *kosher* and *nonkosher*—will no longer apply in Jerusalem. Everything in the city will be *kosher*—no matter how humble or mundane its use. As it says in Zechariah 14,

> In that day there will be inscribed on the bells of the horses, "HOLY TO THE LORD." And the cooking pots in the LORD's house will be like the bowls before the altar. And every cooking pot in Jerusalem and in Judah will be holy to the LORD of hosts....And there will no longer be a Canaanite [a merchant] in the house of the LORD of hosts in that day. (14:20–21 NASB)

No one will be allowed any longer to exploit the service of God's house for personal profit.

Final Scene:
One King over All the Earth

> And the LORD will be king over all the earth; in that day the LORD will be the only one, and His name the only one. (14:9 NASB)

God's original pattern of theocratic government will be extended over all nations. With Jerusalem as His earthly center, Christ will rule as King over the whole earth. Following the pattern of Melchizedek—the king-priest who ruled Jerusalem in the days of Abraham (see Genesis 14:18–20)—Christ will unite in His own Person the two sacred functions of king and priest.

As King, Christ will also be the supreme Judge. One of His first acts will be to summon all nations before Him for judgment:

> But when the Son of Man comes in His glory, and all the angels with Him, then He will sit on His glorious throne. And all the nations will be gathered before Him; and He will separate them from one another, as the shepherd separates the sheep from the goats; and he will put the sheep on His right, and the goats on the left. (Matthew 25:31–33 NASB)

There will be one clear principle of separation between the "sheep" nations and the "goat" nations—the way they have treated the Jews during their period of persecution under antichrist.

To the *sheep*, those who have showed mercy to the Jews at this time, Christ will say:

Come, you who are blessed of My Father, inherit the kingdom prepared for you from the foundation of the world....Truly I say to you,
to the extent that you did it to one of these brothers of Mine, even the
least of them, you did it to Me.   (Matthew 25:34, 40 NASB).

To the *goats*, those who refused to show mercy to the Jews, Christ will say:

Depart from Me, accursed ones, into the eternal fire which has been
prepared for the devil and his angels....Truly I say to you, to the extent
that you did not do it to one of the least of these, you did not do it to
Me.   (Matthew 25:41, 45 NASB)

The *sheep* nations will then be permitted to take their place in Christ's
kingdom; the *goat* nations will be banished from it.

Christ's kingdom, thus established, will far excel that of Solomon both in
the measure of its glory and in the extent of its blessings. As the great drama
in three acts comes to its close, we see all the nations that are left on earth
coming regularly to Jerusalem to share in the blessings of the kingdom and to
join with Israel in celebrating the Feast of Tabernacles. (See chapter 14, verses
16–21.)

What These Prophecies Mean for Us Today

Concerning the Old Testament prophecies of the Lord's return, the apostle Peter wrote to the early Christians, "We have also a more sure word of
prophecy; whereunto ye do well that ye take heed, as unto a light that shineth
in a dark place, until the day dawn, and the day star arise in your hearts" (2
Peter 1:19). For the unbeliever, the world around is getting darker. In the fact
of multiplying pressures and problems, world leaders grope in vain for enduring solutions. For the believer, however, the light of prophetic revelation, like a
lamp, shines more brightly by contrast with the surrounding darkness.

Peter compared the effect of these prophecies to the rising of the "daystar"
within our hearts. He took his metaphor from the action of the planet Venus.
At certain seasons, the daystar, or morning star, rises in the eastern sky immediately before the sun itself comes up over the horizon. At times this "star" is
so bright that it partially dispels the surrounding darkness. It thus becomes
the sun's forerunner, giving assurance—to all who understand its message—
that the sun is ready to appear.

So it is with us as we give careful heed to prophetic truth. Like the "day star" arising in our hearts and dispelling the surrounding darkness, there comes an unshakable inner assurance: *the Lord will soon appear.*

Faith of this kind is not a mystical escape from reality. On the contrary, it is based on proven experience. At a conservative estimate, more than half the prophecies of Scripture concerning Israel and Jerusalem have already been exactly and literally fulfilled—often in defiance of all human estimates of probability. Only unreasoning prejudice would reject, without very careful examination, the thesis that the remaining prophecies will be fulfilled in like manner.

The 1911 edition of the *Encyclopædia Britannica* contains an article by a German professor called Nöldeke on the pronunciation of Hebrew. In the course of the discussion he utterly discounts "the possibility that a Jewish empire will ever again be established in the Middle East." Within less than fifty years, of course, the very thing that the learned professor had dismissed as an absurd improbability was an accomplished fact of history!

The divine commentary on this is given by Isaiah:

[The Lord] turneth wise men backward, and maketh their knowledge foolish; [He] confirmeth the word of his servant, and performeth the counsel of his messengers; [He] saith to Jerusalem, Thou shalt be inhabited; and to the cities of Judah, Ye shall be built, and I will raise up the decayed places thereof.   (Isaiah 44:25–26)

Likewise the psalmist David said,

The Lord nullifies the counsel of the nations; He frustrates the plans of the peoples. The counsel of the Lord stands forever, the plans of His heart from generation to generation.   (Psalm 33:10–11 NASB)

In the face of all unbelief and opposition, the Lord's plan for the restoration of Israel and Jerusalem will be fulfilled—*phase by phase*—just as He has revealed it through his prophets.

ABOUT THE AUTHORS

Derek Prince

Derek Prince (1915–2003) was born in Bangalore, India, into a British military family. He was educated as a scholar of classical languages (Greek, Latin, Hebrew, and Aramaic) at Eton College and Cambridge University in England and later at Hebrew University, Israel. As a student, he was a philosopher and self-proclaimed atheist. He held a fellowship in Ancient and Modern Philosophy at King's College, Cambridge.

While in the British Medical Corps during World War II, Prince began to study the Bible as a philosophical work. Converted through a powerful encounter with Jesus Christ, he was baptized in the Holy Spirit a few days later. This life-changing experience altered the whole course of his life, which he thereafter devoted to studying and teaching the Bible as the Word of God.

Discharged from the army in Jerusalem in 1945, he married Lydia Christensen, founder of a children's home there. Upon their marriage, he immediately became father to Lydia's eight adopted daughters—six Jewish, one Palestinian Arab, one English. Together the family saw the rebirth of the state of Israel in 1948. In the late 1950s the Princes adopted another daughter while he was serving as principal of a college in Kenya.

In 1963 the Princes immigrated to the United States and pastored a church in Seattle. Stirred by the tragedy of John F. Kennedy's assassination, he began to teach Americans how to intercede for their nation. In 1973 he became one of the founders of Intercessors for America. His book *Shaping History through Prayer and Fasting* has awakened Christians around the world to their responsibility to pray for their governments. Many consider underground translations of the book as instrumental in the fall of communist regimes in the USSR, East Germany, and Czechoslovakia.

Lydia Prince died in 1975, and Derek married Ruth Baker (a single mother to three adopted children) in 1978. He met his second wife, like his first, while he was serving the Lord in Jerusalem. Ruth died in December 1998 in Jerusalem where they had lived since 1981.

Until a few years before his own death in 2003 at the age of eighty-eight, Prince persisted in the ministry God had called him to as he traveled the world, imparting God's revealed truth, praying for the sick and afflicted, and sharing his prophetic insights into world events in the light of Scripture. He wrote over forty-five books, which have been translated in over sixty languages and distributed worldwide. He pioneered teaching on such groundbreaking themes as generational curses, the biblical significance of Israel, and demonology.

Derek Prince Ministries, with its international headquarters in Charlotte, North Carolina, continues to distribute his teachings and to train missionaries, church leaders, and congregations through its worldwide branch offices. His radio program, *Keys to Successful Living* (now known as *Derek Prince Legacy Radio*), began in 1979 and has been translated into over a dozen languages. Estimates are that Derek Prince's clear, nondenominational, non-sectarian teaching of the Bible has reached more than half the globe.

Internationally recognized as a Bible scholar and spiritual patriarch, Derek Prince established a teaching ministry that spanned six continents and more than sixty years. In 2002 he said, "It is my desire—and I believe the Lord's desire—that this ministry continue the work, which God began through me over sixty years ago, until Jesus returns."

Lydia Christensen Prince

Lydia Christensen Prince (1890–1975) was born in North Jutland, at the northern tip of Denmark, the youngest of four sisters in an affluent family. Her father was a successful builder who played an important role in developing their hometown of Bronderslev.

Lydia became a teacher in the state school system of Denmark and was a pioneer in the field of home economics. By 1925 she had obtained a post as director of home economics in a large new school in the town of Korsor. While seeking more meaning for her life, she started reading the Bible and received a vision of Jesus Christ that led to her salvation and baptism in the Holy Spirit. After months of earnest prayer and waiting upon God, she became convinced that God was asking her to give up her position as a teacher and go to Jerusalem in the tumultuous days before Israel became a nation.

In October 1928, at the age of thirty-eight, she set out for Jerusalem with about $200 in traveler's checks, no mission or church to support her, and no idea of what she was to do when she arrived. She soon established herself there, learned Arabic, and founded a children's home, becoming the cherished "mother" to dozens of Jewish and Arab orphans, mainly girls, eight of whom became her own children. She also began ministering the gospel to Arab women and later to the British soldiers who visited Jerusalem during their furloughs in World War II.

In the mid-1940s, she met and married Derek Prince, a philosophy and language scholar who was serving in the British army and was stationed in Jerusalem. They ministered there together until the birth of the State of Israel in 1948 when they moved to England with their eight girls.

The Princes served congregations, taught, and ministered while living in England, Africa (where they adopted their ninth daughter), Canada, and the United States. After settling in Fort Lauderdale, Florida, they began traveling internationally as Derek preached and taught the Bible in many nations of the world. Throughout these years, Lydia took care of their family, worked tirelessly and faithfully alongside Derek in their ministry, and even returned to her home economics roots when they were in Africa, teaching home economics to the African women students.

Following a stroke and a two-year illness, Lydia Prince died in October 1975. Her passing was deeply mourned by her family and thousands of people worldwide from a wide variety of backgrounds whose lives she had touched in her nearly fifty years of enthusiastic, energetic, and compassionate ministry.